TINY BUDGET
Cooking

LIMAHL ASMALL

MEALPLANS · SHOPPING LISTS · INGREDIENT SWAPS

bluebird
books for life

Contents

Introduction

Hey guys,

I've spent the last 10 years eating my way to budget-food happiness and now I want to share my knowledge with you. I'm on a mission to show you that good, fresh home-cooked food is easy and fun to make, and – most importantly – can be personalized to your taste buds and lifestyle. All you need is a simple kitchen, this cookbook and the confidence to give things a go, and you'll be feasting on delicious meals each week, all made on a tiny budget.

If there's one thing I can tell you, it's that a smaller shopping bill does not have to mean loss of quality or flavour. The recipes in this cookbook use a variety of meat, fresh veg and tantalizing flavours – all available at good supermarkets.

Nutrition is so important for body and mind, and this book loosely follows an 80:20 rule: 80% of the time you'll be feasting on balanced nutritious food and, well, for the other 20%, let's just say we all need the occasional heap of fluffy pancakes or a hot chicken and cheddar melt!

From my research, I've found there are four main obstacles to cooking delicious meals every day. These are: money, time, confidence and knowledge. You may find one or more of these are stopping you from eating well. This cookbook tackles each of these issues, setting you up for a lifetime of good food.

Whether you're looking to save money, waste less or stop playing the dreaded 'What's for dinner?' game, these flexible mealplans, dedicated shopping lists and step-by-step recipes can simplify your life.

See you in the kitchen,

Limahl xX

THE MEALPLANS

As you may know, the best way to simplify your food life is to plan ahead, so I've started you off with four weekly plans to use in any order. I've tried to keep the Monday to Friday meals fast and easy, and the weekend meals are a little more elaborate. To save you time and money we'll use my Cook Once Eat Twice approach, meaning you can make more at dinner to transform into a new meal for lunch. You'll never eat the same thing two days running, and I think you'll be surprised at how useful this tool is.

If you're busy and your plans often change, I suggest choosing recipes from three or more days of a weekly mealplan to fit around your schedule. Chances are that you'll be at home for a few days each week, and following a flexible mealplan will save you time and effort after a long day.

That's not to say you can't dip in and out, choosing recipes as you would with a traditional cookbook. However, if you are looking to feast within a tiny budget, give the mealplans a go.

SHOPPING LISTS

Inside this cookbook you'll find weekly shopping lists which you can use to follow the mealplans. The idea is to shop once a week and use the fresh ingredients over the seven days rather than purchasing daily, or for each meal. This way you'll use up all the fresh ingredients and build up a decent cupboard of long-life spices and dry goods.

In case you didn't want to carry your book around the supermarket, I've put the lists online and you can print them off from **www.tinybudgetcooking.com/lists.**

It's a big ask to cook breakfast each morning, so I've split the shopping lists into two. The

first list is for lunch and dinners only and you might like to buy some cereal, toast, oats or fruit and yoghurt for very quick breakfasts. The second list is the additional ingredients you would need to follow the complete Breakfast, Lunch and Dinner plan. It's achievable if you've got around 20–30 minutes to cook and eat breakfast each morning. Easy for some, impossible for others! Either way, you'll find plenty of simple breakfast inspiration throughout the cookbook.

If you're wondering how to save money while doing the weekly shop, check out Top 10 Tiny Budget Tips (see pages 10–12).

SWAPSHOP

The good news is that these recipes aren't set in stone. They're adaptable, flexible and can be personalized to suit your taste buds. When using the cookbook, you'll notice there are two ingredients columns: the first is for my original recipe, which you can follow as is, and the second is a column of swappable ingredients. If you don't have an ingredient or just don't like one, you can swap it for one of my suggestions and it'll still taste delicious.

SIMPLICITY

All of the recipes in this cookbook have been tested for ease of use, with clear step-by-step instructions and short simple processes. I've kept the kitchen equipment to the bare essentials, but if you're unsure what you need, head to my website where I've prepared a quick list. It's good to note you don't have to buy the best, just go for the highest quality you can comfortably afford. A little quality could last a lifetime.

Out of 100 delicious recipes, 85 take only 5–30 minutes to prepare and cook. I've also included 15 lip-smacking longer recipes for when you have a little more time – think big hearty beef stews, North African tagines, chicken tray bakes and succulent Thai green curries. These are definitely worth the extra effort.

If I can pass on one bit of advice, it is to enjoy yourself and take a light-hearted approach to cooking. Remember to smile and forgive yourself when things don't go to plan, it's completely normal to make mistakes and you'll soon get into the swing of things – effortlessly planning, shopping and eating your way to budget-food happiness.

SOCIAL GIVING CAMPAIGNS

There were over one million three-day emergency food parcels given out in the UK last year, and an estimated 13 million people in the UK, 43 million in the US, and 1 in 10 Europeans living near the poverty line. I believe it is 100% necessary for businesses to make a positive impact and help people to live more fulfilling lives.

I'm committed – along with my publisher – to getting this cookbook in front of the people who need it most. We're running a fantastic One For One model for the first print run, where for each print edition sold, we are donating a digital cookbook to someone facing food poverty.

Top 10
TINY BUDGET TIPS

1.
WHERE TO SHOP

Many of us don't live near a supermarket and will make frequent trips to the local corner shop throughout the week. I agree we should all support our local shops, but if you are on a tight budget, making that one weekly trip to a large supermarket will bring down the cost of your food bill and give you a better choice of own-brand ingredients. You can always shop locally if you missed something – in cities, head to your local fruit and veg market as you'll often pick up fresh produce cheaper than at the supermarkets.

2.
WHEN TO SHOP

Ask when supermarkets discount produce, then search out the reduced-price aisle for meats with a day left on their 'use by date'. These meats are perfect eaten straight away or for buying in bulk and freezing for up to 3 months. Freeze immediately, then, once defrosted, use them on the same day.

Don't go food shopping when hungry. It's been proven that you'll end up spending more – usually on stuff you don't need.

3.
CHECK THE PRICE

An excellent way to save money is to compare the 'per kg' price and choose the cheaper option.

This is an especially good tip when deciding between packaged or loose vegetables, as you're likely to find the loose veg cheaper. It's also better for the planet; less packaging equals fewer mountains of landfill waste.

Pre-trimmed vegetables or pre-grated cheese will certainly be more expensive. Why buy these when you can do this at home in seconds? Add it all up and you could easily save £100 a year.

4.
BUY OWN-BRAND

It's totally possible to eat and drink premium quality, without the price tag. In blind taste tests the cheaper supermarket own-brand versions often come up trumps against the household names and are winning some major awards. It's all a matter of brand loyalty – many times the only difference between basic and premium goods is the packaging and marketing budget. If in doubt, compare the ingredients and go for the one with less sugar, sweeteners and e-numbers.

If you're into drinks, budget supermarkets have a fantastic selection of award-winning wines and spirits. Search online to find out more.

5.
BUY IN BULK

If your weekly budget can stretch to it, buy bigger packs of long-life ingredients such as rice, canned goods, frozen produce and toilet paper.

This can often reduce the per-portion price, and unlike fresh ingredients they will not spoil before you get around to using them. If you live in shared accommodation, why not join together and bulk-buy household items? This is a good way to save money.

6.
BUY IN SEASON

The good news is that when fruit and vegetables hit peak production they are often lowered in price. From carrots to courgettes, cucumbers to parsnips, if you shop seasonally you will save money! Seasonal produce grown locally will also save on air-freight miles which reduces the impact on the planet. That's win-win!

7.
COOK ONCE EAT TWICE

Once you get into the swing of it, cooking extra for the next day (or to freeze for later) will become second nature. It really will save you time and money and keep you from purchasing those dry meal deals. A friend of mine recently worked out he'd save around £96,000 over his working life by taking a packed lunch to work. That's retirement a few years early!

8.
BUY BIG FLAVOURS

Budget cooking is all about the clever use of ingredients. It's a game of flavour combinations, where the addition of 'big flavours' can transform recipes from mundane into mouth-watering. A good tip is to identify the big flavours that you like, make a list and start adding these ingredients into your recipes.

If you cook like this, expensive meat doesn't have to be the centre of a meal. You can use less and still eat well.

BIG FLAVOURS
eggs / chicken, veg or beef stock / butter
olive oil / sesame oil / bacon / chorizo
feta / white onion / garlic / fresh coriander
spring onion / fresh ginger / fresh chilli / lemon
lime / sundried tomato / olives / capers
soy sauce / tinned sardines / peanuts / mustard
tahini paste / ketchup / honey / salt and pepper
tandoori spice / tikka spice / garam masala
Chinese five spice / ground coriander
cinnamon powder / chilli flakes / dried thyme
dried rosemary / coconut milk

9.
MAKE MEAT GO FURTHER

Love meat? Me too, but before you buy the popular cuts, consider that there are equally (if not more) delicious cuts at a cheaper price. Chicken thighs, for example, are more succulent than breast, contain bones which are great for soups and stocks, and have beautiful skin, which you can grill until crisp. Beef shin and brisket are brilliant slow cooked in soup and stews, and if you can find it, pick up some cooking bacon – it's just the pieces that are the wrong size to be packaged normally. They're available in big supermarkets and are sold on the cheap.

One good way to get meat to go further is to make vegetables and grains the centre of meals and keep meat as a supporting ingredient. Many cultures enjoy meat like this – why not consider trying it out?

10.
LOVE YOUR FREEZER

There are many ways your humble freezer can simplify the way you eat. Not only can you create your own ready-meals, you can split large meat packs, control portions and store food for longer. Here are some tips on how to love your freezer.

★ **BACON AND SAUSAGES** Split packs of bacon and sausages into portions and freeze 2–4 per bag. Defrost in the microwave or in the fridge before cooking.

★ **BONELESS PORK LEG (AND OTHER LARGE MEATS)** Buy around 1kg of meat and cut into 6 pieces. Freeze two pieces for two people (around 350g per bag).

★ **CHICKEN THIGHS OR DRUMS** Split the pack into portions and freeze two pieces per bag.

★ **BREAD** Slice bread and transfer to the freezer. Just pop it into the toaster to defrost.

★ **SPINACH, PEAS, CORN, FRESH HERBS** These contain all the nutrients and will not spoil in the freezer.

★ **CURRY PASTES** Make a batch of fresh Thai green curry paste (page 160) and make takeaway-quality meals in the time it takes for them to be delivered.

★ **OTHER THINGS TO FREEZE** bread / chopped onion / garlic / fresh ginger chilli / chicken stock / soups / sauces pizza dough / bread dough / pie dough par-boiled and seasoned potatoes, for roasting mashed potato / milk / butter / grapes / juices fresh fruit / cooked fruit

FREEZING LIKE A PRO

★

Buy plastic takeaway containers with lids and freezerproof sandwich bags with ties.

★

Remember to label your freezer bags and containers with the contents and dates.

★

As a general rule, freeze items for up to 3 months and use the oldest items first.

★

Cool cooked food before freezing. Aim to get the food into the freezer within two hours of cooking.

★

Defrost food in the fridge. Get into the habit of taking the food out of the freezer and putting it into the fridge before bed. It'll be ready to cook by tomorrow's dinnertime. A good rule of thumb is to use the defrosted food within 24 hours.

★

Always make sure food cooked from frozen is piping hot before eating, and once defrosted, never re-freeze.

★

BREAKFAST	LUNCH	DINNER	
SHAKIN' SHAKSHUKA	CREAMY SAUSAGE, MUSHROOM AND SPINACH SPAGHETTI	HUMMUS MEZZE BOWL	DAY 1
THREE-MINUTE MORNING SMOOTHIE	MEDITERRANEAN HUMMUS BAGUETTE	HONEY-GLAZED BEEF NOODLES WITH GREEN BEANS	DAY 2
SWEET POTATO BREAKFAST HASH	SUNDRIED TOMATO FRITTATA	GRILLED MACKEREL AND BUTTERED BABY POTATOES	DAY 3
FLUFFY PANCAKES WITH CREAM CHEESE AND BLUEBERRIES	SMOKED MACKEREL SALAD WITH LEMON YOGHURT DRESSING	TANDOORI WHOLE ROAST CAULIFLOWER WITH RAITA AND COUS COUS	DAY 4
SAVOURY FRENCH TOAST WITH GARLIC BUTTER	SPICED CAULIFLOWER SOUP	LUCKY CHICKEN BAKE	DAY 5
SINGAPORE-STYLE EGG ON TOAST	CHICKEN AND CHEDDAR MELT	MEATBALL MARINARA	DAY 6
BREAKFAST NAAN	SWEET POTATO AND SUNDRIED TOMATO SOUP	RED DHAL WITH CUMIN-CRUSTED POTATOES	DAY 7

Use the leftover hummus and a little chutney from yesterday's dinner

Whizz up half of the roast tandoori cauliflower from yesterday's dinner

Save two of the chicken thighs from yesterday's chicken bake

It takes just minutes to make your own naan bread

Make use of the infused oil that comes in your jar of sundried tomatoes

What's in Store?

THIS WEEK'S MEALPLAN will take you on a journey across the globe. You'll find gorgeous marinades and warm spices from the Middle East; tantalizing aromas and the rich depth of flavour from India; juicy tomatoes, succulent chicken and soft butter beans from Italy; and the mouth-watering soy, garlic and ginger trinity from Asian cooking.

One of my favourites this week is the Meatball Marinara (see page 44). You can make incredibly light and juicy meatballs from pork sausages and cannellini beans in only 30 minutes. You've got to try them! I've also included a couple of comfort classics, because we all need the occasional treat – anyone for fluffy blueberry pancakes and creamy sausage spaghetti?

The lists opposite include all you need to make recipes for two people for a week. Don't forget to read my Top 10 Tiny Budget Tips on pages 10–12 before you go shopping, as they can help you save money. Basic ingredients are not included in these shopping lists so make sure you always have chicken, beef or vegetable stock cubes, salt and pepper, caster sugar and olive oil at home.

Happy cooking!

LUNCH AND DINNER

FRESH PRODUCE

1 apple
★ 2kg baby potatoes
1 head of broccoli
1 carrot
1 large cauliflower
★ 900g cherry tomatoes
80g coriander
1 courgette
½ cucumber
★ 4 bulbs of garlic
8cm piece of fresh ginger
300g green beans
2 lemons
300g mushrooms
★ 1kg onions
3 peppers (mixed colours)
180g spinach leaves
★ 1 bunch of spring onions
★ 1kg sweet potatoes

MEAT AND DAIRY

★ 8 rashers of bacon
250g beef mince
★ 350g cheddar
4 chicken thighs, skin-on
  and bone-in
★ 200g cream cheese
★ 6 free-range eggs
6 pork sausages
250g smoked mackerel
★ 500g Greek yoghurt
★ 250g salted butter

STORE CUPBOARD

2 packs of large (30cm)
  par-baked baguette
1 x 400g tin of butterbeans
1 x 400g tin of cannellini
  beans
1 x 400g tin of chickpeas
★ 37g cumin seeds
200g egg noodles
★ 1.5kg self-raising flour
★ 300g clear honey
★ 500g red lentils
★ 150ml soy sauce
★ 500g spaghetti
★ 280g sundried tomatoes
★ 110g tandoori spice
2 x 400g tins of chopped
  tomatoes
★ 500g cous cous

★ Starred ingredients will not be finished this week and can go towards the breakfast recipes (to supplement the below), or towards another week.

BREAKFAST

FRESH PRODUCE

2 bananas
200g blueberries
180g spinach leaves

MEAT AND DAIRY

12 free-range eggs
2 pints whole milk

STORE CUPBOARD

400g sliced bread
12g mixed herbs
1 x 400g tin of chopped
  tomatoes
35ml vanilla essence

BREAKFAST

LUNCH

SHAKIN' SHAKSHUKA

SERVES 2 | READY IN 20 MINS | VEGETARIAN

INGREDIENTS

1 tbsp olive oil
1 small onion, cut into
  1–2cm cubes
½ pepper (any colour), chopped
  into 1–2cm cubes
1 clove garlic, minced
1 x 400g tin of chopped tomatoes
2 tsp tandoori spice
4 eggs
salt and pepper
2 slices of buttered toast,
  to serve (optional)

SWAP SHOP

–
2 spring onions, cut into
  1–2cm slices
½ courgette, chopped into
  1–2cm cubes
¼ tsp garlic powder
8 peeled tomatoes, chopped
1 tsp each cumin and paprika
200g tofu
–

–

1. Heat the olive oil in a non-stick frying pan over a medium heat. Cook the onion, pepper and garlic for 5 minutes, or until the pepper is softening.

2. Add in the tomatoes and tandoori spice and give it all a good stir. Make four small indents in the mixture and then gently crack an egg into each hole. Season with salt and pepper.

3. Cook for 10–15 minutes until the egg whites are no longer translucent. You could place a lid on the pan to speed up the cooking time by a couple of minutes. Serve on its own or with hot buttered toast.

ADDITIONS

1 tsp chilli flakes / 2 tbsp coriander, chopped
2 tbsp feta, crumbled / 2 sundried tomatoes
1 spring onion, finely chopped

CREAMY SAUSAGE, MUSHROOM AND SPINACH SPAGHETTI

SERVES 2 | READY IN 20 MINS

INGREDIENTS

2–3 sausages
1 tsp olive oil
1 onion, finely diced
1 clove garlic, minced
2 portions of spaghetti (about 100g
  per person)
salt and pepper
3–5 mushrooms, roughly chopped
75–100g cream cheese
handful of spinach leaves, roughly
  chopped

SWAP SHOP

6 sundried tomatoes
–
2 spring onions, finely sliced
¼ tsp garlic powder
2 portions of pasta or rice

–
½ leek, roughly chopped
75ml double cream
handful of steamed kale

> No mushrooms? No worries; it will taste delicious without

1. Bring a medium saucepan of water to the boil. Meanwhile, remove the skin from the sausages and roughly chop into 1–2cm chunks.

2. Heat the olive oil in a non-stick frying pan over a medium heat. Add the onion, garlic and sausage pieces and begin to fry.

3. Add the spaghetti to the boiling water, throw in a pinch of salt and give it a stir. Cook the spaghetti for 10–12 minutes, or according to the packet instructions.

4. Once the sausage meat has begun to brown, add the mushrooms to the pan and stir together. Place a lid or plate over the frying pan and steam-cook the mixture for 5 minutes.

5. Add the cream cheese plus a good pinch of pepper and a small pinch of salt. Stir until the cream cheese has melted, then add the spinach to the frying pan. Drain the spaghetti, mix it through the sauce and serve hot.

ADDITIONS

1 tbsp pine nuts / 2 rashers of bacon, sliced
1 tbsp grated parmesan or cheddar

HUMMUS MEZZE BOWL

SERVES 2 | READY IN 1 HR
PLUS MAKING THE HUMMUS AND CHUTNEY
COOK ONCE EAT TWICE:
Mediterranean Hummus Baguette
(Day 2, Lunch, see page 26)

INGREDIENTS	SWAP SHOP
1 quantity Hummus (see page 158)	–
1 quantity Spiced Tomato Chutney (see page 160)	–
salt and pepper	–
1 tbsp coriander, chopped (optional)	–
bread, to serve (optional)	–

For the sweet potato fries

1 sweet potato, cut into long 1cm-thick chips	1 large potato, cut into long 1cm-thick chips
2 tsp olive oil	–
1 tsp flour	–
1 tsp mixed herbs (optional)	–

For the Mediterranean vegetables

1 pepper (any colour), cut into long 1cm-thick sticks	1 red onion, roughly sliced
1 carrot, cut into long 1cm-thick sticks	100g green beans, left whole
1 courgette, cut into long 1cm-thick sticks	200g mushrooms, roughly chopped
1 tsp olive oil	–
2 cloves garlic, chopped	2cm fresh ginger, grated

For the beef koftas

125g beef mince	125g pork mince
½ onion, grated	¼ tsp onion powder
½ clove garlic, grated	¼ tsp garlic powder
½ tsp tandoori spice	½ tsp tikka spice
1 tsp olive oil	–

Save time tomorrow – prepare your Mediterranean Hummus Baguette tonight (see page 26)

1. Follow the instructions on pages 158 and 160 to make quantities of Hummus and Spiced Tomato Chutney. It takes 1 hour to cook the chutney, so I recommend making that first while you prepare the other ingredients.

2. To make the sweet potato fries, turn the grill onto a medium heat. Put the sweet potato chips in a baking tray and toss with the olive oil. Add the flour, a good pinch of salt and the mixed herbs, if using. Toss again to coat the fries, then place them under the grill for 30–35 minutes, turning midway through the cooking time.

3. Meanwhile, make the Mediterranean vegetables. Add the pepper, carrot and courgette to a large saucepan along with the olive oil, garlic and a good pinch of salt. Stir together and put on a low heat until ready to serve.

4. While the vegetables are frying, make the beef koftas. Add the beef mince, grated onion and garlic to a medium bowl. Add the tandoori spice plus a pinch of salt and pepper. Use your hands to stir and mash the mixture together, and then shape eight to ten mini beef koftas, each about 3cm long. Set aside.

5. Heat 1 teaspoon of olive oil in a non-stick frying pan over a medium-hot heat. Fry the beef koftas for 6 minutes, until cooked through.

6. Reserving at least 2 tablespoons for tomorrow's lunch (Day 2, Lunch, page 26), spread the Hummus around the inside of the two bowls. Pile on the sweet potato fries and the beef koftas.

7. Reserving 125g for tomorrow's lunch (Day 2, Lunch, page 26), divide the Mediterranean vegetables between the two bowls. Serve with a large spoonful of the Spiced Tomato Chutney, as well as some coriander and bread, if you like.

You can
make this veggie
by serving with
pan-fried halloumi
slices instead of
the beef koftas

DINNER

LUNCH

BREAKFAST

DINNER

THREE-MINUTE MORNING SMOOTHIE

SERVES 2 | READY IN 3 MINS | VEGETARIAN

INGREDIENTS

500ml whole milk
2 soft and ripe bananas

2 tsp vanilla essence

EQUIPMENT

stick blender

SWAP SHOP

500ml oat or coconut milk
3 juicy ripe peaches, peeled
  and chopped
1 tsp honey

ADDITIONS

1 tsp honey / 3 ice cubes

1. Add the milk, bananas and vanilla essence to a blender. Blend until smooth and frothy, and enjoy! If you don't have a standing blender, you can also transfer your ingredients to a large bowl and use a stick blender to blitz the ingredients together.

MEDITERRANEAN HUMMUS BAGUETTE

SERVES 2 | READY IN 10 MINS | VEGETARIAN

COOK ONCE EAT TWICE:
Hummus Mezze Bowl
(Day 1, Dinner, see page 22)

INGREDIENTS

1 large par-baked baguette
2 tbsp Hummus (see page 158)
2 tbsp Spiced Tomato Chutney
  (see page 160)
125g leftover Mediterranean
  vegetables (see page 22)
4 sundried tomatoes, chopped
1 tbsp coriander, leaves only
  (optional)

SWAP SHOP

4 slices of bread
2 tbsp grated cheddar
1 tomato, sliced

1 courgette, chopped
  and pan-fried
8 olives, halved

–

1. If you are using a par-baked baguette, wet your hands and rub them on the baguette to create a nice crust, then follow the packet instructions to bake the baguette until golden brown. Cut it in half lengthways. (Any other bread or toast will also taste good.)

2. Spread the Hummus on one half of the baguette and the Spiced Tomato Chutney on the other half.

3. Pile the leftover vegetables on top of the Hummus, then layer with the sundried tomatoes and coriander, if using.

4. Sandwich the two pieces together and use a sharp serrated knife to cut the baguette in half. Serve up your masterpiece or wrap it in foil and take it to work for lunch.

Get ahead by making the Sundried Tomato Frittata for tomorrow's lunch (see page 30)

HONEY-GLAZED BEEF NOODLES WITH GREEN BEANS

SERVES 2 | READY IN 15 MINS

INGREDIENTS

1 spring onion, finely chopped

2 cloves garlic, minced

2cm fresh ginger, minced (optional)

2 tbsp soy sauce

1 tbsp honey

1 tbsp olive oil

300g green beans, cut into 2cm batons

125g beef mince

2 portions of egg noodles (about 100g per person)

SWAP SHOP

½ onion, finely chopped

–

–

2 tbsp oyster sauce

1 tbsp caster sugar

–

1 pepper and 1 carrot, cut into 2cm batons

125g pork, chicken or tofu, thinly sliced, or prawns

2 portions of rice noodles or spaghetti (about 100g per person)

1. Bring a small saucepan of water to the boil. In a large bowl, make the sauce by adding the spring onion, a quarter of the garlic and ginger (if using), the soy sauce, honey and ½ tablespoon of the olive oil. Beat together with a fork until the honey has dissolved.

2. Add the chopped green beans to a frying pan with the remaining olive oil, garlic, ginger and the beef mince. Stir to break up the mince and gently fry over a medium-low heat. Add the egg noodles to the pan of boiling water and cook for about 5 minutes, or according to the packet instructions.

3. When the noodles are cooked, drain well and toss them in the bowl of sauce. Pour the noodles and sauce into the frying pan and mix together with the beef and green beans. Serve hot.

ADDITIONS

60g peanuts / handful of coriander

½ tsp chilli flakes / 2 tbsp sesame seeds

LUNCH

BREAKFAST

DINNER

SWEET POTATO BREAKFAST HASH

SERVES 2 | READY IN 15 MINS | VEGETARIAN

INGREDIENTS

1 sweet potato, cut into 1cm cubes
2 tsp olive oil
1 onion, diced
1 clove garlic, minced
6 cherry tomatoes, halved
½ tsp mixed herbs
salt and pepper
handful of spinach leaves
1–2 tsp lemon juice
chilli flakes (optional)

SWAP SHOP

1 potato, cut into 1cm cubes
–
–
1 tbsp chopped chives
1 pepper, roughly chopped
½ tsp thyme
–
handful of kale
2 tsp lime juice
–

1. Bring 600ml water to the boil in a deep saucepan. Turn the heat up and keep the water gently bubbling. Place the sweet potato in the water and boil for 5–7 minutes, until soft.

2. Heat the olive oil in a non-stick frying pan over a medium-low heat. Add the onion and garlic and sauté for 3–4 minutes. Stir in the tomatoes and the mixed herbs.

3. Drain the sweet potato and add it to the frying pan. Toss together with a good pinch of salt and pepper and continue to sauté for another 2 minutes.

4. Stir in the spinach until it has wilted, then top with the lemon juice and a pinch of chilli flakes, if using. Serve.

ADDITIONS

1 tbsp pine nuts / 2 rashers of crispy bacon
2 fried eggs / chilli sauce
2 sundried tomatoes, chopped

SUNDRIED TOMATO FRITTATA

SERVES 2 | READY IN 15 MINS | VEGETARIAN

INGREDIENTS

3 eggs
salt and pepper
3 tbsp grated cheddar
1 tbsp sundried tomato oil
  (taken from the jar below)
1 small onion, diced
6 mushrooms, cut into 1–2cm
  pieces
4 sundried tomatoes, diced

SWAP SHOP

–
–
50g goat's cheese, crumbled
1 tbsp olive oil

2 spring onions, diced
½ courgette, cut into
  1–2cm pieces
2 rashers of bacon, diced

1. Crack the eggs into a bowl and add a good pinch of salt and pepper. Add the cheddar into the bowl and whisk with a fork until combined.

2. Add the sundried tomato oil into a non-stick ovenproof frying pan and fry the onion over a medium heat for 2 minutes. Add the mushrooms and sundried tomatoes and cook for another 2 minutes. Turn the grill on to a medium-hot heat.

3. Spread the ingredients evenly in the pan, then pour the egg and cheese mixture over the top. Cook gently for 5–6 minutes before cooking under the grill for 2–3 minutes.

4. If you don't have a grill, place a lid or plate over the frying pan and lower the heat. Cook for 10–12 minutes, or until the top is no longer liquid. Serve.

ADDITIONS

1 tsp mixed herbs / 1 clove garlic, minced
green salad or spinach leaves, to serve

GRILLED MACKEREL AND BUTTERED BABY POTATOES

SERVES 2 | READY IN 30 MINS

COOK ONCE EAT TWICE:
Smoked Mackerel Salad with Lemon Yoghurt Dressing
(Day 4, Lunch, see page 35)

INGREDIENTS

1kg skin-on baby potatoes,
   cut into 3cm chunks
salt and pepper
8 cherry tomatoes

1 tsp olive oil
125g smoked mackerel
   (about half the pack)
1 head of broccoli, cut into
   3cm florets
3 tbsp butter
½ tbsp lemon juice
1 spring onion, finely chopped

SWAP SHOP

6–8 medium potatoes, peeled
   and cut into 3cm chunks
–

1 pepper, cut into
   3cm pieces
–

125g smoked herring

2 courgettes, cut
   into 3cm chunks
–

–
¼ red onion, finely chopped

> You can peel and thinly chop the broccoli stalk too, and use it raw in a salad

1. Bring a large, deep saucepan of water to the boil. Turn the heat up and keep the water gently bubbling.

2. Add the potato chunks to the water. Throw in a good pinch of salt and boil for 20 minutes, or until they are cooked through.

3. Put on your kettle to boil and turn the oven on to 220°C (fan 200°C/gas mark 7).

4. Add the cherry tomatoes to an ovenproof dish, drizzle the olive oil over the top and add a pinch of salt and pepper. Place the mackerel on top and cook in the oven for about 10 minutes.

5. With 5 minutes to go, place the broccoli in a medium saucepan and cover with boiling water. Place a lid on and simmer for 3–4 minutes until tender. Drain the broccoli, then add it back into the saucepan along with 1 tablespoon of the butter, the lemon juice and a pinch of salt. Shake together to coat the broccoli then place a lid on the pan until you're ready to serve.

6. Drain the potatoes, then add them back into the same saucepan along with the remaining butter, the spring onion and a good pinch of salt and pepper. Crush each potato using the back of a spoon and stir together to coat in the butter.

7. Serve the mackerel and tomatoes with the potatoes and broccoli, reserving half the vegetables for tomorrow's lunch (Day 4, Lunch, page 35).

ADDITIONS

2 tbsp pine nuts / 1 tbsp capers
1 tbsp sultanas / 2 tbsp parsley

BREAKFAST

LUNCH

FLUFFY PANCAKES WITH CREAM CHEESE AND BLUEBERRIES

SERVES 2 | READY IN 20 MINS | VEGETARIAN

INGREDIENTS

100g cream cheese
1 egg
1 tbsp caster sugar
1 tsp vanilla essence
salt
220ml whole milk

140g self-raising flour

zest of 1 lemon (optional)
100g blueberries, plus extra
 for serving
2 tbsp butter

SWAP SHOP

100g ricotta cheese
–
1 tbsp honey
zest of 1 lemon
–
220ml oat milk
 or almond milk
140g plain flour, plus 1 tsp
 bicarbonate of soda
–
100g fruits of the forest,
 plus extra for serving
–

1. If you want to serve all the pancakes in one go, preheat your oven to 160ºC (fan 140ºC/gas mark 3).

2. Place a large bowl on the kitchen surface and add the cream cheese, egg, sugar, vanilla essence, a pinch of salt and the milk. Whisk together until smooth.

3. Add in the self-raising flour and the lemon zest, if using. Whisk again until a luxuriously thick, lump-free batter has formed.

4. Gently crush the blueberries and add them to the batter.

5. Melt 1 teaspoon of butter in a non-stick frying pan over a medium heat. Pour 60ml or a small ladleful of batter into the pan – it will spread to form a 10–12cm pancake. Cook for 1–3 minutes until the top surface is no longer liquid, then flip with a spatula and cook the other side for about 1 minute.

6. Stack the pancakes in the warm oven, or eat them one by one. Sprinkle with the extra blueberries, and serve.

ADDITIONS

2 tbsp Greek yoghurt, to serve
honey, to serve

SMOKED MACKEREL SALAD WITH LEMON YOGHURT DRESSING

SERVES 2 | READY IN 20 MINS

COOK ONCE EAT TWICE:
Grilled Mackerel and Buttered Baby Potatoes
(Day 3, Dinner, see page 31)

INGREDIENTS

leftover buttered potatoes (see
  page 31), cut into 1–2cm slices
leftover cooked broccoli (see page
  31), cut into 1–2cm slices
125g smoked mackerel
  (about half the pack), shredded
4 cherry tomatoes,
  cut into quarters
½ spring onion, finely sliced
¼ cucumber, cut into
  1cm cubes
3 tbsp Greek yoghurt
½ tbsp olive oil
½ tbsp lemon juice
salt and pepper

SWAP SHOP

3 cooked beetroots,
  cut into 1–2cm slices
80g watercress

125g smoked herring,
  shredded
½ pepper (any colour),
  roughly chopped
1 tbsp minced red onion
½ pepper (any colour),
  roughly chopped
3 tbsp mayonnaise
—
½ tbsp cider vinegar
—

1. Add the leftover potatoes and broccoli, shredded mackerel, cherry tomatoes and spring onion into a large bowl and gently mix together.

2. Place the cucumber into a separate bowl. Add the yoghurt, olive oil, lemon juice and a good pinch of salt and pepper, stirring to mix it all together.

3. Mix the yoghurt dressing through the mackerel salad and toss to coat the ingredients. Enjoy!

ADDITIONS

1 cooked beetroot, cubed / 1 tbsp capers
1 tbsp pine nuts / 2 boiled eggs, halved
1 raw broccoli stem, chopped

TANDOORI WHOLE ROAST CAULIFLOWER WITH RAITA AND COUS COUS

SERVES 2 | READY IN 1 HR | VEGETARIAN

COOK ONCE EAT TWICE:
Spiced Cauliflower Soup
(Day 5, Lunch, see page 39)

INGREDIENTS

1 large cauliflower
3 tbsp Greek yoghurt
2½ tsp tandoori spice
2 cloves garlic, minced
salt and pepper
100g cous cous
½ pepper (any colour),
  finely chopped
½ tbsp lemon juice

For the raita

4 tbsp Greek yoghurt
¼ clove garlic, crushed
¼ cucumber, finely diced
1 tsp olive oil
1 tsp lemon juice

SWAP SHOP

–
3 tbsp plain yoghurt
2½ tsp tikka spice
–
–
100g rice
2 tomatoes, finely
  chopped
–

–
–
–
–
–

1. Preheat the oven to 220°C (fan 200°C/gas mark 7). Choose a large saucepan that's big enough to hold the whole cauliflower, and fill it with water. Bring it to the boil, turn the heat to medium and keep the water bubbling gently.

2. Remove the leaves from the cauliflower, then cut the stalk flat so it sits steady on the kitchen surface. Locate the base of the core on the bottom of the cauliflower and use a small sharp knife to carefully hollow out a cone shape, about 3cm deep. This technique considerably speeds up the cooking time.

3. Plunge the cauliflower top down into the water so it is completely submerged. Place the lid on top and boil for 5 minutes, then remove the cauliflower and leave it to dry on an oven tray for 5 minutes.

4. Add the yoghurt to a bowl along with 2 teaspoons of tandoori spice, the garlic and a good pinch of salt and pepper. Stir together, then liberally smooth the marinade all over the cauliflower.

5. Roast the cauliflower in the middle of the oven for 45 minutes. With 10 minutes to go, make the raita in a separate bowl. Combine the yoghurt with the garlic, cucumber, olive oil, lemon juice and a pinch of salt and pepper.

6. With 5 minutes to go, pour the cous cous into a bowl and add the remaining tandoori spice. Pour boiling water over the top until it reaches 1cm above the cous cous. Cover with a plate and leave for 5 minutes.

7. Stir the chopped pepper and lemon juice through the cous cous and divide it between the two plates.

8. Carve the roasted cauliflower into two halves, and set one aside for tomorrow's lunch (Day 5, Lunch, see page 39). Cut the other half in two and share between the two plates, topped with cucumber raita.

Marinate in spiced yoghurt to gently flavour the dish

LUNCH

BREAKFAST

SAVOURY FRENCH TOAST WITH GARLIC BUTTER

SERVES 2 | READY IN 15 MINS | VEGETARIAN

INGREDIENTS

2–3 cloves garlic, minced
2 tbsp butter
4 slices of slightly stale bread
100g cheddar, grated
2 eggs
2 tbsp whole milk
1 spring onion, finely chopped
salt and pepper
1 tsp olive oil

SWAP SHOP

2 spring onions, chopped
2 tbsp olive oil
–
100g brie or camembert
–
2 tbsp water
¼ red onion, finely chopped
–
–

1. Place the garlic and butter in a bowl and mix together until combined. If the butter is cold, heat it for no more than 8 seconds in a microwave, or mash until soft with the back of a fork. Lay out the slices of bread and spread the garlic butter on one side of each slice.

2. Divide the grated cheese between 2 slices of bread, and sandwich the other slices on top.

3. Crack the eggs into a bowl, add the milk, half the spring onion and a good pinch of salt and pepper. Beat together to combine, then pour the mixture into a large shallow dish.

4. Heat the olive oil in a non-stick frying pan over a medium heat, then soak both sides of each sandwich in the egg mixture for 10 seconds. Pan-fry each sandwich for 3 minutes on each side until golden. Serve hot, sprinkled with the remaining spring onion.

ADDITION

2 tbsp parsley, chopped

SPICED CAULIFLOWER SOUP

SERVES 2 | READY IN 30 MINS

COOK ONCE EAT TWICE:
Tandoori Whole Roast Cauliflower with Raita and Cous Cous (Day 4, Dinner, see page 36)

INGREDIENTS

1 tsp olive oil
1 onion, diced
1 clove garlic, minced
½ leftover roasted cauliflower (see page 36), cut into 2cm pieces
1–2 baby potatoes, cut into 2cm pieces
½ tsp tandoori spice
1 chicken stock cube
salt and pepper

SWAP SHOP

–
–
–
2 parsnips, roasted and cut into 2cm pieces
1 carrot, cut into 2cm pieces
1½ tsp tikka spice
1 vegetable stock cube
–

EQUIPMENT

stick blender

1. Put on your kettle to boil. Add the olive oil to a saucepan with the onion and garlic and fry over a medium heat for 2 minutes.

2. Add the leftover cauliflower and potatoes to the saucepan along with the tandoori spice and 100ml water. Steam-fry for 3 minutes before adding the stock cube and stirring until dissolved.

3. Pour in 500ml boiling water and simmer for 10 minutes until the potatoes are soft. Remove the pan from the heat and blend with a stick blender until smooth. Season with salt and pepper and gently stir through. Serve.

ADDITIONS

2 slices of crusty bread / 1 tsp tandoori spice handful of beetroot crisps

Great for feeding large groups – simply double up the quantities

LUCKY CHICKEN BAKE

SERVES 2 | READY IN 30 MINS

COOK ONCE EAT TWICE:
Chicken and Cheddar Melt
(Day 6, Lunch, see page 43)

INGREDIENTS

1 x 400g tin of butterbeans
3 cloves garlic, minced
2 onions, cut into quarters
3 rashers of bacon, roughly
  chopped
1 x 400g tin of chopped tomatoes
salt and pepper
1 pepper (any colour), chopped
  into 3cm pieces
4 chicken thighs, skin-on
  and bone-in
2 tsp olive oil
100g cous cous
1 chicken stock cube, crushed

SWAP SHOP

1 x 400g tin of kidney beans
–
–
10cm chorizo, roughly
  chopped
6–8 large tomatoes
–
6–8 mushrooms, roughly
  chopped
4 chicken breasts, skin-on
–
–
–

1. Preheat the oven to 210ºC (fan 190ºC/
gas mark 6).

2. Drain and rinse the butterbeans and
add them to a large oven tray or baking dish
along with the garlic, onion, bacon, chopped
tomatoes, a good pinch of pepper and the
pepper pieces.

3. Thoroughly mix everything together and
place the chicken thighs skin-side up on top
of the veg. Drizzle a little of the oil over the
chicken skin and season with salt and pepper.

4. Bake in the middle of the oven for about
40–45 minutes. The chicken skin will turn
crisp and golden and the veg soft and juicy.

5. Place the cous cous in a bowl, add the
chicken stock cube and pour over enough
boiling water to reach about 1cm above
the grains. Stir together and cover for
5 minutes until soft and fluffy.

6. Serve up the bake, reserving two chicken
thighs and 1 mugful of the vegetables and
sauce to make tomorrow's lunch (Day 6,
Lunch, see page 43).

ADDITIONS

3 sundried tomatoes / 2 tsp mixed herbs
8 olives, chopped

DINNER

BREAKFAST

LUNCH

SINGAPORE-STYLE EGG ON TOAST

SERVES 2 | READY IN 10 MINS | VEGETARIAN

INGREDIENTS

2 eggs
2 handfuls of spinach
  leaves
1 tbsp butter
2 slices of toast
2 tbsp soy sauce

SWAP SHOP

–
2 handfuls of kale or
  spring greens
–
–
–

1. Bring a medium saucepan of water to the boil, then lower the heat to a gentle simmer. Carefully lower 2 eggs into the water using a spoon and cook them for 5 minutes.

2. Remove the eggs with a spoon and place them under cold running water for 30 seconds.

3. Take the pan from the heat and pour most of the boiling water out, leaving just 1 tablespoon in the bottom of the pan. Add the spinach, cover and set aside.

4. Gently tap and roll each egg on a flat surface to crack the shell, then carefully peel them. By now the spinach should have wilted – if not, turn the heat on and gently stir until the leaves wilt.

5. Butter the toast, cut it into strips and divide between the two bowls. Drain the spinach and arrange on top with a halved egg and a drizzle of the soy sauce. Serve.

ADDITIONS

½ tsp white pepper or chilli flakes
½ tsp sesame oil / ½ spring onion, chopped
1 tbsp coriander, chopped

CHICKEN AND CHEDDAR MELT

MAKES 2 SUBS | READY IN 15 MINS
COOK ONCE EAT TWICE:
Lucky Chicken Bake
(Day 5, Dinner, see page 40)

INGREDIENTS

1 large par-baked baguette
chicken and sauce leftovers
  from Lucky Chicken Bake
  (see page 40)
100g cheddar, grated

SWAP SHOP

bread of your choice
–

100g pizza mozzarella, sliced

Wrap this
in kitchen foil
to enjoy on
the go

1. If you are using a par-baked baguette, wet your hands and rub them on the baguette to create a nice crust, then follow the packet instructions to bake the baguette until golden brown. Cut it in half lengthways. (Any other bread or toast will also taste good.)

2. Slice and finely shred the two leftover chicken thighs. Discard the bones and mix the shredded meat through the leftover vegetables and sauce. Divide this mixture between the baguette pieces.

3. Top each baguette with the grated cheese. Place the baguettes on an oven tray and grill on a medium heat for 3–5 minutes, until the cheese has melted. Enjoy your masterpiece.

ADDITIONS

2 sundried tomatoes, chopped
4 olives, chopped

MEATBALL MARINARA

SERVES 2 | READY IN 30 MINS

INGREDIENTS

1 x 400g tin of cannellini beans, drained and rinsed

4 cloves garlic

1 x 400g tin of chopped tomatoes

1 bay leaf (optional)

salt and pepper

1 rasher of bacon, roughly chopped

3 pork sausages

½ onion, grated

1 egg

2 tbsp flour

1 tbsp olive oil

2 portions of spaghetti (about 100g per person)

2 tbsp grated cheddar, to serve (optional)

SWAP SHOP

1 x 400g tin of butterbeans, drained and rinsed

–

300g cherry tomatoes, chopped

–

–

2 sundried tomatoes

3 chicken sausages

1 spring onion, chopped

–

–

–

–

–

Light and juicy meatballs in a bacon-infused marinara sauce

1. Bring a large saucepan of water to the boil and keep the water gently bubbling.

2. Squash a few of the cannellini beans between your fingers; if they are hard, gently heat them for 2 minutes in a frying pan with 2 tablespoons of water. Add the beans to a large bowl.

3. Mince 3 of the garlic cloves. Pour the tomatoes into a small saucepan, add the bay leaf (if using), minced garlic, a big pinch of salt and the bacon. Turn the heat to medium-low and leave to cook.

4. Mash the beans with your fingers to make a paste. Remove the sausage meat from the casings and place it in the bowl with the onion and a pinch of salt and pepper. Grate in the remaining garlic clove, crack in the egg and mix it all together with a spoon to make a moist mixture.

5. Cover a plate with a thin layer of flour. Form golf-ball-sized balls with floured hands and place them on the floured plate. Heat the olive oil in a non-stick frying pan over a medium-hot heat. Carefully place each ball into the pan and fry for 12 minutes, turning carefully every 2–3 minutes.

6. Halfway through the cooking time, place the spaghetti in the boiling water. Add a pinch of salt and cook for 10–12 minutes.

7. When the meatballs have had their cooking time, lower the heat. If you have used the bay leaf, remove it from the sauce. Pour the sauce on top of the meatballs, then place a lid or plate over the pan to keep them warm.

8. Toss together the spaghetti and meatballs and divide between two plates. Serve hot.

DINNER

LUNCH

BREAKFAST

BREAKFAST NAAN

**SERVES 2 | READY IN 10 MINS
PLUS MAKING THE NAANS**

INGREDIENTS

INGREDIENTS	SWAP SHOP
2 x 12-minute Naans (see page 162)	–
1 tsp olive oil	–
4 rashers of bacon	–
2 eggs	4 sundried tomatoes
2 tbsp Spiced Tomato Chutney (see page 160)	2 tsp hot sauce
2 tbsp coriander, leaves only (optional)	–

1. Make two 12-minute Naans, as shown on page 162.

2. Meanwhile, heat the olive oil in a large non-stick frying pan over a medium heat. Add the bacon and fry for 2 minutes. Crack in the eggs, flip the bacon and fry it all until the egg white has set and the bacon is crisp.

3. Spread 1 tablespoon of the Spiced Tomato Chutney on each naan and top with the bacon, eggs and coriander, if using. Serve.

ADDITION

1 garlic clove, minced

SWEET POTATO AND SUNDRIED TOMATO SOUP

SERVES 2 | READY IN 25 MINS

INGREDIENTS

INGREDIENTS	SWAP SHOP
1 tbsp sundried tomato oil (from the jar from Day 3), plus extra for drizzling	1 tbsp tomato puree
1 onion, diced	–
2 cloves garlic, minced	–
1 chicken stock cube	1 vegetable stock cube
1½ sweet potatoes, cut into 3cm cubes	200g red lentils
salt and pepper	–
1 tbsp crumbled feta (optional)	–

EQUIPMENT

stick blender

1. Heat the sundried tomato oil in a saucepan over a medium-hot heat. Add the onion and garlic, frying for 3–4 minutes until soft.

2. Add 750ml boiling water to the saucepan along with the stock cube and the chopped sweet potatoes. Simmer on a medium heat for 15–20 minutes, or until the sweet potato is soft.

3. Blitz the soup with a stick blender, taste test and season with salt and pepper.

4. Divide between two bowls and drizzle with sundried tomato oil. Top with the feta, if you like.

ADDITIONS

1 rasher of crispy bacon / 1 tsp lemon juice
1 tbsp crème fraiche

DINNER

RED DHAL WITH CUMIN-CRUSTED POTATOES

SERVES 2 | READY IN 45 MINS

INGREDIENTS

INGREDIENTS	SWAP SHOP
1 onion, diced	–
2 cloves garlic, minced	–
2cm fresh ginger, minced	–
½ tsp cumin seeds	–
1 tbsp olive oil	–
2–3 cherry tomatoes, chopped	1 tbsp tomato puree
2 tsp tandoori spice	2 tsp tikka spice
1 chicken stock cube	1 vegetable stock cube
200g red lentils	200g brown lentils
salt and pepper	–
2 tbsp coriander, chopped (optional)	–

For the cumin-crusted potatoes

6–8 baby potatoes	–
3 cloves garlic, finely chopped	–
3 spring onions, finely chopped	–
2cm fresh ginger, finely chopped	–
small handful of chopped coriander	–
1 tsp cumin seeds	–
1 tsp tandoori spice	–
1 tbsp butter	–
1 tbsp olive oil	–

1. Put on your kettle to boil. Add the onion, garlic and ginger to a saucepan along with the cumin seeds, oil and chopped tomatoes. Fry over a medium heat for 3 minutes before adding the tandoori spice and about 100ml water. Stir together for 2 minutes to release the flavours from the spices.

2. Crumble in the stock cube, add the lentils and pour in 625ml boiling water. Boil vigorously for 5 minutes, then lower the temperature and leave to gently bubble for 30–35 minutes. Stir occasionally and add a small amount of water if it becomes too thick.

3. Meanwhile, make the cumin-crusted potatoes. Bring a large deep saucepan of water to the boil. Cut the baby potatoes into equal-sized pieces and boil for 15–20 minutes until they are cooked. Drain and leave to dry.

4. Make the fresh mix by combining the garlic, spring onions, ginger and coriander in a bowl.

5. Make the dry mix by placing the cumin seeds on a chopping board. Gently crush and chop with a knife to make a rough powder. Add the powder to a separate bowl with the tandoori spice and a pinch of salt and pepper.

6. Melt the butter and olive oil in a non-stick frying pan over a medium-hot heat. Add the potatoes and fry for 3 minutes before adding the dry mix. Toss and fry for a further 6 minutes before adding in the fresh mix. Stir-fry for a final 4 minutes, then pile the cumin-crusted potatoes into two bowls and top with your rich red dhal.

BREAKFAST	LUNCH	DINNER	
BREAKFAST CRUMBLE WITH APPLE AND HONEY	BUTTERBEAN AND CHORIZO SOUP	ROAST CHICKEN WITH BOULANGERE POTATOES	DAY 1
SMASHED AVOCADO ON TOAST	PEA SOUP WITH CHEESE CROUTONS	CHICKEN IN SPRING GREENS	DAY 2
GREEK YOGHURT POTS	TIPH'S CHICKEN NOODLE SOUP	STICKY PORK AND AUBERGINE	DAY 3
SAVOURY PORRIDGE OATS WITH SUNFLOWER SEEDS	STICKY PORK BURRITO	CHICKEN, LEEK AND ORZO PIE	DAY 4
EGG AND COURGETTE ROLL-UPS	ASIAN SLAW WRAPS	ORZO, PORK AND PEAS	DAY 5
SIMPLE QUESADILLA	SPINACH AND FETA SPANAKOPITA	PANGRATTATO BREADCRUMB SPAGHETTI	DAY 6
TOMATO BRUSCHETTA	PAN-FRIED POTATO AND SWEETCORN CAKES WITH HONEY MUSTARD SLAW	MY KIND OF PAELLA	DAY 7

Use the roast chicken from Day 1 to make two dishes

Save the pork from yesterday's dinner to make this lunch

... AND use the roast chicken from Day 1 to make this pie

What's in Store?

THIS WEEK'S MEALPLAN shows you how to cook four recipes from one roast chicken. It also includes my mate Jeff's buttery Boulangère Potatoes, which are slowly baked in chicken stock and a little fresh spinach.

Pangrattato Breadcrumb Spaghetti (see page 76) is a real winner for vegetarians. Pangrattato is a piquant mixture of pan-fried breadcrumbs, lemon zest and garlic that coats the spaghetti and gives a real kick to this simple recipe. It's also known as 'poor man's parmesan' and is a great substitute for vegetarians and vegans. Sprinkle it over pasta and veg to bring them to life.

I recommend making a big batch of the Granola (see page 166) at the start of this week. It will keep well in a sealed container for a couple of weeks and makes a delicious breakfast or snack.

Don't forget to read the tips section on pages 10–12 before you go shopping as they'll really help you to save money. As with last week, basic ingredients are not included in the list so make sure you always have chicken, beef or vegetable stock cubes, salt and pepper, caster sugar and olive oil.

Happy cooking!

LUNCH AND DINNER

FRESH PRODUCE

1 aubergine
1 head of broccoli
3 carrots
700g cherry tomatoes
25g coriander
3 bulbs of garlic
★ 6cm piece of fresh ginger
1 large leek
3 lemons
1 lime
1kg onions
★ 25g parsley
1kg frozen peas
3 peppers (mixed colours)
2.5kg potatoes
1 small red cabbage
360g spinach leaves
★ 250g spring greens
2 bunches of spring onions
★ 1 small white cabbage

MEAT AND DAIRY

★ 250g salted butter
350–400g cheddar
225g chorizo
200ml crème fraiche
★ 12 free-range eggs
★ 200g feta
6 pork shoulder steaks
(600g in total)
whole chicken (1.4–1.7kg)
1 x 270g pack of filo pastry

STORE CUPBOARD

5 bay leaves
★ 800g loaf of bread
1 x 400g tin of butterbeans
★ 12g chilli flakes
★ 200ml hoisin sauce
★ 300ml clear honey
100g English mustard
★ 500g orzo pasta
★ 300g peanut butter
★ 500g rice
★ 300g rice noodles
★ 150ml soy sauce
★ 500g spaghetti
★ 1 x 150g tin of sweetcorn
★ 500g paella rice
★ 6 plain tortilla wraps

★ Starred ingredients will not be finished this week and can go towards the breakfast recipes (to supplement the below), or towards another week.

BREAKFAST

FRESH PRODUCE

3 apples
1 avocado
25g basil
1 courgette
500g frozen forest fruits

MEAT AND DAIRY

500g Greek yoghurt

STORE CUPBOARD

500g porridge oats
100g sunflower seeds
150–200g mixed fruit
and nut

BREAKFAST

LUNCH

DINNER

BREAKFAST CRUMBLE WITH APPLE AND HONEY

SERVES 2 | READY IN 15 MINS
PLUS MAKING THE GRANOLA | VEGETARIAN

INGREDIENTS

4 tbsp Granola
  (see page 166)
3 apples, peeled and chopped
  into 2–3cm pieces
1 tsp honey
yoghurt or crème fraiche (optional)

SWAP SHOP

4 tbsp toasted sunflower seeds
  (see tip, below)
3 pears, peeled and chopped
  into 2–3cm pieces
1 tsp caster sugar
–

> Substitute granola for toasted sunflower seeds: pan-fry 4 tablespoons seeds until golden, drizzle with honey and allow to cool

1. Follow the instructions on page 166 to make a batch of Granola.

2. Add the apples to a small pan along with the honey and 3 tablespoons of water. Cover and cook over a medium heat for 10 minutes or until the apples are soft. Mash them a little with a fork, then divide between two bowls.

3. Stir 2 tablespoons of granola into each bowl and serve with a spoonful of yoghurt or crème fraiche, if you like.

ADDITIONS

½ tsp vanilla essence
½ tsp ground cinnamon

BUTTERBEAN AND CHORIZO SOUP

SERVES 2 | READY IN 20 MINS

INGREDIENTS

12cm chorizo, peeled
1 onion, diced
2 cloves garlic, minced
1 tbsp olive oil
1 x 400g tin of butterbeans,
  drained and rinsed
2 tbsp parsley, chopped
3cm lemon peel
1 chicken stock cube
salt and pepper

SWAP SHOP

2 sausages
½ bulb fennel, sliced
¼ tsp garlic powder
–
1 x 400g tin of cannellini beans,
  drained and rinsed
1 tsp mixed herbs
–
1 vegetable stock cube
–

> If you can't find chorizo, pan-fry slices of chicken or pork sausages

1. Put on your kettle to boil. Very finely mince 2cm of the chorizo and add it to a bowl with the onion and garlic.

2. Cut the remaining chorizo into 5mm slices and add to a dry saucepan. Fry over a medium heat for 2–3 minutes until the chorizo has released its oils and is almost golden in colour, then transfer to a plate and set aside. Fry the onion, garlic and minced chorizo in the oil for 3–4 minutes.

3. Add the butterbeans, half of the chopped parsley and the lemon peel. Stir together and pour in 600ml water and the stock cube. Bring to the boil, then lower the heat and simmer for 3 minutes.

4. Garnish with the remaining chopped parsley, black pepper and the reserved cooked chorizo.

ADDITIONS

½ tsp ground paprika / 2 slices of crusty bread

ROAST CHICKEN WITH BOULANGERE POTATOES

SERVES 2 | READY IN 1 HR 30 MINS

INGREDIENTS

INGREDIENTS	SWAP SHOP
2 onions	–
3 cloves garlic	3 tbsp chives
2 bay leaves	1 tsp dried thyme or rosemary
salt and pepper	–
1 whole chicken (about 1.4–1.7kg)	–
3 tbsp olive oil	–
5 medium potatoes, cut into 5mm slices	3–4 sweet potatoes, cut into 5mm slices
3 tbsp butter	9 tsp goose fat
handful of spinach leaves	handful of kale
1 chicken stock cube	–
10 cherry tomatoes	4 tomatoes

EQUIPMENT
18–21cm ovenproof dish

COOK ONCE EAT FOUR TIMES:
Chicken in Spring Greens (Day 2, Dinner, see page 61)
Tiph's Chicken Noodle Soup (Day 3, Lunch, see page 63)
Chicken, Leek and Orzo Pie (Day 4, Dinner, see page 69)

1. Preheat the oven to 210ºC (fan 190ºC/ gas mark 6) and put on your kettle to boil.

2. Finely slice one of the onions and crush two of the garlic cloves. Add them to a large baking tray along with the bay leaves. Pour in 250ml water and season generously with salt and pepper.

3. Place the chicken on top of the onion. Rub the skin with 1 tablespoon of the olive oil and season with salt and pepper.

4. Place the chicken in the middle of the oven for around 1 hour 20 minutes (for a 1.5kg bird). After 30 minutes, turn the bird over so it's skin-side down, and after 1 hour flip it over again so it's skin-side up. This ensures succulent meat and a nice crisp skin.

5. Finely slice the remaining onion and the final garlic clove. To begin layering the boulangère potatoes, spread a few slices of onion and garlic in the ovenproof dish. Dot 1 tablespoon butter over the top, and add a pinch of salt and pepper, a few leaves of spinach and a layer of potatoes. Then repeat the layering process, finishing with a layer of potatoes on the top.

6. Dissolve the stock cube in 150ml boiling water. Pour the stock on the potatoes. Drizzle 1 tablespoon of olive oil over the top and bake in the oven for 1 hour.

7. With 10 minutes remaining, toss the cherry tomatoes in 1 tablespoon of olive oil. Season with a little salt and pepper and roast in a small ovenproof dish until the potatoes are ready.

8. When the chicken has cooked, remove it from the oven and let it rest for up to 10 minutes before serving.

9. Serve one breast, half the tomatoes and a quarter of the potatoes per person. Reserve all the leftovers and the chicken carcass for more recipes.

ADDITIONS FOR THE BOULANGERE POTATOES
½ tsp dried thyme / ½ tsp dried rosemary
2 rashers of bacon, chopped

BREAKFAST

LUNCH

DINNER

SMASHED AVOCADO ON TOAST

SERVES 2 | READY IN 10 MINS | VEGETARIAN

INGREDIENTS

1½ tsp olive oil
2 eggs
salt and pepper
1 ripe avocado
2 slices of bread
butter (optional)
¼ tsp chilli flakes

SWAP SHOP

–
–
–
4 tbsp cottage cheese
2 crumpets
–
¼ tsp black pepper

1. Heat 1 teaspoon of olive oil in a non-stick frying pan over medium-hot heat. Crack in the eggs, season with salt and pepper and gently fry until the whites are no longer liquid. If you like a runny yolk, stop cooking here or continue until the yolks are set.

2. Meanwhile, cut the avocado in half and discard the stone and skin. Scoop out the flesh, roughly chop it into small pieces and place in a bowl along with a pinch of salt and pepper and the remaining olive oil. Use the back of a fork to mash it into a paste.

3. Pop two slices of bread into the toaster, and when ready you can either butter the toast or use the runny yolk as a butter substitute! Pile on the egg and avocado and season with chilli flakes.

ADDITIONS

2 tsp chilli sauce / 1 tbsp grated cheddar
2 rashers of crispy bacon

PEA SOUP WITH CHEESE CROUTONS

SERVES 2 | READY IN 12 MINS

INGREDIENTS

400g frozen peas

2 chicken stock cubes
3 cloves garlic
1½ tbsp butter
2 onions, diced
2 tbsp olive oil
2 slices of bread, cut into
  1–2cm cubes
4 tbsp grated cheddar
salt and pepper

EQUIPMENT
stick blender

SWAP SHOP

1 head broccoli, roughly
  chopped
2 vegetable stock cubes
3 tbsp chives
1½ tbsp olive oil
2 shallots, diced
–
2 slices of baguette, cut into
  1–2cm cubes
4 tbsp grated parmesan
–

1. Put on your kettle to boil. Pour 1.2 litres of boiling water into a large bowl along with the frozen peas and the chicken stock cubes.

2. Finely dice two of the garlic cloves. Melt the butter in a large saucepan over a medium heat. Add the onion and garlic and fry for 3 minutes.

3. Add the peas and stock to the saucepan and heat for 5 minutes without allowing to boil.

4. Meanwhile, heat the olive oil in a non-stick frying pan over a medium heat. Gently squash the final garlic clove and add it to the pan, then throw in the bread cubes and stir-fry for 3–4 minutes, until golden.

5. Sprinkle the grated cheddar over the bread cubes and season with salt and pepper. When the cheese has melted, remove the croutons from the pan and leave to cool on a plate. Discard the squashed garlic clove.

6. Thoroughly blend the soup with a stick blender until smooth and serve with the croutons.

CHICKEN IN SPRING GREENS

SERVES 2 | READY IN 10 MINS

COOK ONCE EAT TWICE:
Roast Chicken with Boulangère Potatoes
(Day 1, Dinner, see page 57)

INGREDIENTS

leftover boulangère potatoes (see
  page 57)
250g spring greens, hard stalk
  removed and finely shredded
salt and pepper
75–100ml crème fraiche
100g leftover roast chicken,
  shredded (see page 57)

SWAP SHOP

300g buttered baby
  potatoes
250g savoy cabbage,
  finely shredded
–
100ml double cream
100g cooked chicken, shredded

1. Put on your kettle to boil. Reheat the boulangère potatoes in a microwave (or in the oven, preheated to 200°C/fan 180°C/gas mark 6 for 15–20 minutes).

2. Place the shredded spring greens in a saucepan and cover with boiling water. Add a pinch of salt and boil for 3–5 minutes, until soft. Drain well and return to the saucepan.

3. Pour in the crème fraiche and shredded chicken. Stir in a good pinch of salt and pepper and heat through for 3–4 minutes before serving on top of the hot potatoes.

ADDITION
2 slices of crusty bread

Reserve the remaining chicken meat and carcass in the fridge for the next day

BREAKFAST

LUNCH

GREEK YOGHURT POTS

SERVES 2 | READY IN 5 MINS | VEGETARIAN

INGREDIENTS

8 tbsp Granola
  (see page 166)
100g frozen fruits of the forest
8 tbsp Greek yoghurt

SWAP SHOP

8 tbsp toasted nuts

100g any berries
8 tbsp plain yoghurt

1. In two small bowls or glasses, layer 2 tablespoons of Granola, then 25g of the fruit, followed by 2 tablespoons of yoghurt.

2. Add another layer of each ingredient to the bowls and eat immediately.

3. You can defrost the frozen fruit the night before but I like to eat from frozen – the berries chill the Greek yoghurt, giving it an ice-cream-like consistency.

ADDITIONS
½ tsp vanilla essence / 1 tsp honey

TIPH'S CHICKEN NOODLE SOUP

SERVES 2 | READY IN 30 MINS

COOK ONCE EAT TWICE:
Roast Chicken with Boulangère Potatoes
(Day 1, Dinner, see page 57)

INGREDIENTS

100g leftover roast chicken (see
  page 57), shredded
4cm fresh ginger, grated
3 cloves garlic, minced
25g coriander
2 spring onions
1½ chicken stock cubes
1 small carrot, cut into batons
25g red cabbage, shredded
handful of spinach leaves
2 portions of rice noodles (about
  100g per person)
1–2 tbsp soy sauce
½ lime, cut into quarters

SWAP SHOP

100g cooked pork or beef

1 ginger tea bag
25g chives
–
–
1½ vegetable stock cubes
25g beansprouts
–
25g pak choi
2 portions of egg noodles (about
  100g per person)
1–2 tbsp Bragg liquid amino
½ lemon, cut into quarters

Swap fresh ginger for a ginger tea bag: simply add it into the stock for 5–10 minutes

1. Put on your kettle to boil. Remove all of the meat from the chicken carcass and reserve the meat for later on in the recipe.

2. Place the chicken carcass into a large saucepan with the ginger, garlic, half of the coriander, 1 trimmed spring onion and the chicken stock cubes.

3. Pour in 1.2 litres boiling water and gently boil the carcass for 25 minutes. The longer you cook the stock, the tastier it will be.

4. Chop the remaining spring onion, then distribute both between two soup bowls along with the remaining coriander, carrot batons, shredded cabbage and spinach.

5. Re-boil the kettle. Add the rice noodles into a large bowl and cover with boiling water. Leave to soften for 5 minutes, then drain and divide the noodles between each soup bowl.

6. After 25 minutes, drain the liquid into a saucepan, pressing down on the ingredients with a spoon to extract all the flavour. Discard the ingredients in the sieve so you are left with a clear stock.

7. Add the shredded chicken to the stock and bring to the boil. Taste test and season with soy sauce and a squeeze of lime. Pour into the bowls, stir together and enjoy!

ADDITIONS
1 chilli, de-seeded and finely chopped
handful of beansprouts / 2 tsp sesame oil
1 tbsp mint, chopped / 1 boiled egg, halved

STICKY PORK AND AUBERGINE

SERVES 2 | READY IN 20 MINS

COOK ONCE EAT TWICE:
Sticky Pork Burrito
(Day 4, Lunch, see page 66)

INGREDIENTS

200g rice

3 pork shoulder steaks (about
    300g)
1 tsp olive oil
1 onion, roughly chopped

3 cloves garlic, finely sliced
1 aubergine, cut into
    3–4cm cubes
1 pepper (any colour), cut into
    3–4cm cubes
100ml hoisin sauce
1 spring onion, chopped
½ tsp chilli flakes (optional)

SWAP SHOP

2 portions of noodles (about
    100g per person)
300g chicken, beef
    or tofu
–

3 spring onions, roughly
    chopped
3 tbsp chopped chives
150g mushrooms, left whole

100g green beans, left whole

75ml black bean sauce

–

–

1. Put on your kettle to boil. Add the rice into a large saucepan and pour in 375ml boiling water. Bring to the boil, then lower the heat, cover the pan and simmer for 15 minutes.

2. Take the pan off the heat and allow it to sit for 5 minutes until the sauce is ready. The rice should absorb all the liquid and become nice and fluffy.

3. Cut the pork shoulder steaks into strips, roughly 2 x 3cm in size. Heat the olive oil in a non-stick frying pan over a medium heat. Add the pork strips to the pan and stir-fry for 5 minutes, until golden.

4. Add the onion and garlic to the pan along with the aubergine and pepper. Pour in 100ml water and the hoisin sauce. Stir together, cover with a lid or plate and cook for 10 minutes.

5. Serve one quarter of the sticky pork and rice per person along with a garnish of spring onion and chilli flakes, if you like. Transform the two additional portions into the Sticky Pork Burrito (Day 4, Lunch, see page 66).

ADDITIONS
2 tbsp coriander, chopped / 1 tsp chilli flakes
small handful of peanuts

DINNER

SAVOURY PORRIDGE OATS WITH SUNFLOWER SEEDS

SERVES 2 | READY IN 15 MINS | VEGETARIAN

INGREDIENTS	SWAP SHOP
2 spring onions, chopped into 5mm pieces, plus extra for garnish	3 tbsp chives, chopped
1 tsp grated fresh ginger	1 ginger tea bag
100g porridge oats	–
3 tbsp sunflower seeds, plus extra to garnish	3 tbsp pumpkin seeds, plus extra to garnish
2 tbsp coriander, chopped	–
1½ tbsp soy sauce	1½ tbsp Bragg liquid amino
black pepper	–

1. Put on your kettle to boil. Add the spring onion and ginger to a small saucepan along with 600ml boiling water and the porridge oats. Stir together and bring to the boil, then reduce the heat to medium-low.

2. Add in the sunflower seeds and continue to stir the porridge (clockwise if you're a traditionalist) for 10 minutes.

3. Stir in the chopped coriander, soy sauce and a good pinch of pepper. Pour into two bowls, top with additional seeds and enjoy.

ADDITIONS

1 tsp sesame oil / 1 tsp chilli flakes
2 fried eggs

STICKY PORK BURRITO

SERVES 2 | READY IN 20 MINS

COOK ONCE EAT TWICE:
Sticky Pork and Aubergine
(Day 3, Dinner, see page 64)

INGREDIENTS	SWAP SHOP
2 plain tortilla wraps	–
2 portions of leftover Sticky Pork and Aubergine (see page 64)	–
100g red cabbage, finely shredded	100g lettuce, shredded
6 cherry tomatoes, cut into quarters	½ pepper (any colour), diced
salt and pepper	–
1 tbsp coriander, leaves only (optional)	–

1. Lay out the wraps and top with a portion of the Sticky Pork and Aubergine along the centre of each.

2. Toss the red cabbage and tomatoes together in a bowl with a pinch of salt and pepper and coriander, if using.

3. Distribute the salad evenly down the centre of each wrap. If you are eating this on the move, tear off some tin foil and place it under each wrap. Roll it up and take it to work.

ADDITIONS

2 tbsp coriander, chopped
small handful of peanuts

BREAKFAST

LUNCH

DINNER

CHICKEN, LEEK AND ORZO PIE

SERVES 2 | READY IN 40 MINS

COOK ONCE EAT TWICE:
Roast Chicken with Boulangère Potatoes
(Day 1, Dinner, see page 57)

INGREDIENTS

50g orzo pasta
1 onion, diced
1 leek, cut into 5mm pieces

1 tbsp olive oil
1 bay leaf
salt and pepper
100g leftover roast chicken (see
  page 57), shredded
50g tinned sweetcorn, drained
1 tsp English mustard
4 tbsp crème fraiche
1 chicken stock cube
2 handfuls of spinach leaves
3 tbsp grated cheddar
3 sheets of filo pastry

1 tbsp butter

EQUIPMENT
18–21cm ovenproof dish

SWAP SHOP

50g rice
3 spring onions
2 sticks celery, cut into 5mm
  pieces
—
1 tsp mixed herbs
—
100g cooked pork, shredded

—
1 tsp wholegrain mustard
50ml water
1 vegetable stock cube
2 handfuls of spring greens
50g parmesan, grated
½ sheet ready-rolled
  puff pastry
—

1. Preheat the oven to 200°C (fan 180°C/
gas mark 6) and put on your kettle to boil.

2. Add the orzo to a small saucepan and
pour in 500ml boiling water. Add a pinch
of salt and simmer for 12–15 minutes, until
al dente.

3. Meanwhile, add the onion and leek to a
large saucepan along with the olive oil, bay
leaf and a pinch of salt and pepper. Cover
and sweat over a medium heat for 5 minutes.

4. Add the shredded chicken, sweetcorn,
mustard and crème fraiche to the pan.
Stir together then add in the stock cube and
150ml boiling water.

5. When the orzo is al dente, drain and
add it to the large pan. Throw in the spinach
and stir until it is wilted. Finally, mix in the
grated cheddar.

6. Taste test and season with salt and pepper
as needed, then pour the mixture into the
oven dish.

7. Take the filo pastry sheets and tear them
in half. Gently scrunch each sheet as if
trying to make a rose and use them to cover
the pie filling. Make sure the sheets are
loosely scrunched so that air can circulate
and help them to crisp up.

8. Heat the butter in the microwave (or in
a pan) and gently spoon the butter over the
pastry. This will ensure it turns beautifully
golden. Bake on a low shelf in the oven for
15 minutes, and then serve.

ADDITION
2 rashers of bacon, roughly chopped

LUNCH

BREAKFAST

DINNER

EGG AND COURGETTE ROLL-UPS

SERVES 2 | READY IN 10 MINS | VEGETARIAN

INGREDIENTS

1 courgette
4 eggs
salt and pepper
2 tsp olive oil
3 tbsp grated cheddar
1 spring onion, finely chopped

SWAP SHOP

2 handfuls of spinach leaves
–
–
2 tsp sundried tomato oil
3 tbsp crumbled feta
1 tbsp chives, finely chopped

1. Grate the courgette then scoop it up and give it a gentle squeeze over the sink to remove the excess liquid.

2. Add two of the eggs to a mug or bowl, whisk together with a fork and season well with salt and pepper.

3. Pour 1 teaspoon of the oil into a non-stick frying pan over a medium-hot heat. When it is hot, pour in the eggs. Rotate the pan to create a large, even omelette, then lower the temperature slightly.

4. As soon as the liquid egg has set, add half of the grated courgette, grated cheddar and spring onion in a line along the pancake.

5. Wait another 20 seconds for the pancake to firm up, then carefully roll it using a spatula and your fingers. Be careful not to touch the hot pan!

6. Turn the roll over every 30 seconds to get the outside nice and golden. Serve to your significant other, then repeat the process for yourself.

ADDITIONS

1 tbsp coriander / 1 rasher of crispy bacon
1 tbsp pine nuts

ASIAN SLAW WRAPS

SERVES 2 | READY IN 12 MINS | VEGETARIAN

INGREDIENTS

¼ red cabbage, finely sliced
¼ white cabbage, finely sliced
1 carrot, grated
2 spring onions, finely chopped
1 pepper (any colour), cut into long thin slices
2 tbsp coriander, chopped
2 tbsp hoisin sauce
3 tbsp peanut butter
1 tbsp lime juice
½ tsp grated fresh ginger
½ tsp grated garlic
2 plain tortilla wraps

SWAP SHOP

200g radishes, finely sliced
1 broccoli stem, finely sliced
1 stick celery, finely chopped
3 tbsp chives
¼ cucumber, cut into long thin slices
2 tbsp parsley, chopped
2 tbsp miso paste
3 tbsp tahini paste
1 tbsp lemon juice
–
–
–

1. Place the cabbage in a large bowl with the grated carrot, half of the chopped spring onion and the pepper slices. Throw in the chopped coriander and mix together.

2. In a separate bowl, add the hoisin sauce, peanut butter, lime juice, grated ginger, grated garlic and the remaining spring onion. Mix together to form a delicious paste.

3. Lay out two wraps and spread the paste equally across both. Pile on the salad and roll up your wraps.

ADDITIONS

100g tofu, pan-fried
100g cooked chicken or pork, shredded

Try this paste as a marinade for grilled chicken

ORZO, PORK AND PEAS

SERVES 2 | READY IN 15 MINS

INGREDIENTS

75g orzo pasta

1½ tbsp butter
1 bay leaf
3 pork shoulder steaks (about 250–300g), cut into 2–3cm pieces
2 cloves garlic, minced
1 chicken stock cube
75g frozen peas
handful of spinach leaves
black pepper
3 tbsp grated cheddar

SWAP SHOP

75g rice or 2 portions of spaghetti
1½ tbsp olive oil
½ tsp rosemary
250–300g chicken, cut into 2–3cm pieces, or quorn pieces
–
1 vegetable stock cube
75g green beans, chopped
handful of spring greens
–
3 tbsp grated parmesan

1. Bring a saucepan of 600ml water to the boil and add the orzo to the pan. Allow it to bubble away for 15 minutes.

2. Meanwhile, add the butter, bay leaf and pork to a non-stick frying pan. Stir-fry over a medium heat for 3 minutes.

3. Add the garlic to the pan and fry for another 3 minutes. Pour in 100ml boiling water and dissolve the chicken stock cube in the pan. Cover with a lid or plate and cook over a low temperature for 7 minutes.

4. One minute before the orzo is ready, add the frozen peas to the saucepan and continue to cook, then drain the orzo and peas and add both to the frying pan with the pork.

5. Add the spinach and stir through until it has wilted. Season with a pinch of pepper, top with the grated cheddar and serve.

SIMPLE QUESADILLA

SERVES 2 | READY IN 10 MINS | VEGETARIAN

INGREDIENTS

2 plain tortilla wraps
1–2 tsp English mustard
100g cheddar, grated

2 tbsp parsley, roughly chopped

SWAP SHOP

2 pitta breads
2 tsp wholegrain mustard
100g goat's cheese,
  crumbled
2 tbsp coriander or basil

1. Place one wrap into a medium-hot griddle or frying pan and heat for 45 seconds to 1 minute. When the underside is golden, flip the wrap over and spread 1 teaspoon of mustard onto the cooked side.

2. Sprinkle half the cheese and parsley evenly over the wrap and then fold it in half. Cook for another 30 seconds, then flip to cook the other side until your desired crunch is achieved. Repeat the process with the second wrap and serve.

ADDITIONS

1 spring onion, chopped
2 slices of ham, chopped

SPINACH AND FETA SPANAKOPITA

SERVES 2 | READY IN 25 MINS | VEGETARIAN

INGREDIENTS

180g spinach leaves, roughly
  chopped
6 spring onions, finely chopped
1 tbsp olive oil, plus 1 tsp
1 x 400g tin of chickpeas
  (optional)
100–150g feta

salt and pepper
3 sheets of filo pastry
1 tbsp butter

SWAP SHOP

180g tinned spinach

1 onion, finely chopped
–
–

150g cottage cheese,
  plus 1 egg
–
3 sheets of Turkish yufka pastry
–

> Using tinned spinach? Place it in a sieve and press the water out before adding to the saucepan

1. Preheat the oven to 200°C (fan 180°C/ gas mark 6). Heat the spinach leaves in a small saucepan over a medium heat until wilted. Transfer to a sieve and press out the liquid with the back of a spoon.

2. Add the spring onions to a saucepan with 1 tablespoon of the olive oil. Fry over a medium heat for 2 minutes until soft.

3. Drain and rinse the chickpeas, if using, and add them to the saucepan with the spinach. Stir until combined, then remove from the heat.

4. Crumble in the feta, and season with salt and pepper.

5. Drizzle 1 teaspoon of the olive oil on the surface of an oven tray. Lay two sheets of the pastry on the tray in a cross formation. Spoon the spinach mixture into the central area where the two pastry sheets cross over.

6. Place a third sheet on top of the filling, then fold all the layers up over the filling and gently twist and scrunch it all together like the end of a Christmas cracker.

7. Melt the butter in the microwave (or in a pan) and spoon it evenly over the pastry to give you a beautiful golden finish.

8. Bake the pie in the lower part of the oven for 15 minutes, then serve.

BREAKFAST

LUNCH

PANGRATTATO BREADCRUMB SPAGHETTI

SERVES 2 | READY IN 20 MINS | VEGETARIAN

INGREDIENTS

salt and pepper
1 slice of bread
3 cloves garlic
zest and juice of 1 lemon
½ tsp chilli flakes (optional)
1 tbsp olive oil, plus extra for
   drizzling
2 portions of spaghetti (about 100g
   per person)
1 head of broccoli, cut into
   2cm florets
1½ tbsp butter
lemon wedges, to serve

EQUIPMENT

stick blender

SWAP SHOP

–
–
3 tbsp chopped chives
–
–
–

pasta of your choice

200g kale, roughly
   shredded
1 tbsp olive oil
–

> Pangrattato is a mix of breadcrumbs, zest and garlic, also known as 'poor man's parmesan'

1. Bring a deep saucepan of water to the boil. Add a pinch of salt.

2. Place the slice of bread in a large bowl and blitz into breadcrumbs with a stick blender.

3. Mince two of the garlic cloves and add them to the bowl along with the lemon zest, ½ teaspoon of salt, a pinch of pepper and the chilli flakes, if using.

4. Heat the olive oil in a non-stick frying pan over a medium heat. Pour in the breadcrumb mix and stir-fry for 3–4 minutes until golden, then transfer to a plate to cool.

5. Add the spaghetti to the saucepan of salted boiling water. Cook for 10–12 minutes, until al dente.

6. Bring another saucepan of water to the boil. With 4 minutes to go on the pasta time, plunge the broccoli florets into the boiling water for 3 minutes, then drain and return to the pan.

7. Drain the spaghetti and add it to the broccoli. Mince the final clove of garlic. Add the butter to the empty spaghetti saucepan, along with the lemon juice, minced garlic and a good pinch of salt and pepper. Toss the spaghetti and broccoli through the sauce, then toss it all in the pangrattato breadcrumbs.

8. Serve with a drizzle of olive oil and a squeeze of lemon to taste.

ADDITION

2 tbsp grated parmesan

DINNER

LUNCH

BREAKFAST

DINNER

TOMATO BRUSCHETTA

SERVES 2 | READY IN 10 MINS | VEGETARIAN

INGREDIENTS

150g cherry tomatoes
salt and pepper
4 tbsp basil, chopped
1 tbsp olive oil
3 slices of bread
1 clove garlic (optional)
2 tbsp olive oil

SWAP SHOP

150g any ripe tomatoes
–
2 tbsp oregano leaves
–
1 baguette
–
2 tbsp sundried tomato oil

1. Slice the cherry tomatoes into small pieces and add to a bowl. Season generously with salt and pepper, 3 tablespoons of the chopped basil leaves and the olive oil. Mix together and set aside.

2. Toast the bread and cut each slice in half. If you fancy it, cut a clove of garlic in half and gently rub the cut end all over the surface of the toast.

3. Drizzle the oil over the bread then top with the tomato mixture. Make sure to pour over the juice as it contains the massive flavour.

ADDITIONS

1 ball of mozzarella, torn
1 slice of prosciutto ham, roughly sliced

PAN-FRIED POTATO AND SWEETCORN CAKES WITH HONEY MUSTARD SLAW

SERVES 2 | READY IN 30 MINS | VEGETARIAN

INGREDIENTS

2 medium potatoes (300–400g), chopped into 3cm pieces
salt and pepper
¼ red cabbage, finely shredded
¼ white cabbage, finely shredded
1 carrot, grated
2 spring onions, chopped
2 tsp honey
1½ tsp English mustard
juice of ½ lemon
3 tbsp olive oil
75g tinned sweetcorn, drained
3 tbsp grated cheddar
1 egg

SWAP SHOP

100g rice

—

200g radishes, roughly chopped
1 broccoli stalk, finely chopped
¼ bulb fennel, finely chopped
5 tbsp chives, chopped
2 tsp caster sugar
1½ tsp wholegrain mustard

—
—
—
—
1 tbsp flour

These cakes freeze well, so make a batch and defrost when required

1. Put on your kettle to boil. Add the potatoes to a saucepan and cover with boiling water. Add a pinch of salt and leave to simmer for 12 minutes, until just cooked.

2. Meanwhile, add the shredded cabbage to a bowl along with the grated carrot and half the chopped spring onions.

3. In a separate bowl, combine the honey, ½ teaspoon of mustard, lemon juice and 1 tablespoon of olive oil. Season with a good pinch of salt and pepper and beat together with a fork until it is thick and luxurious.

4. Drain the potatoes and return them to a dry saucepan. Add the remaining chopped spring onion, sweetcorn, grated cheddar, remaining mustard and a good pinch of salt and pepper.

5. Whisk the egg in a cup or bowl and add to the potatoes. Use a fork to mix and mash it all together. Keep the mixture rough and do not overmix.

6. Heat 1 tablespoon of olive oil in a non-stick frying pan over a medium-hot heat. Use a serving spoon to scoop out 7–8 spoonfuls of the potato mixture. Shape them in your hands, then drop them into the hot oil.

7. Pan-fry the cakes for 8 minutes on one side, then flip them over, add another tablespoon of olive oil and fry for another 4 minutes.

8. Toss the dressing with the salad, and serve on two plates alongside the potato cakes. Enjoy!

MY KIND OF PAELLA

SERVES 2 | READY IN 30 MINS

INGREDIENTS

1 chicken stock cube
100g chorizo
1 tbsp olive oil
1 onion, diced
2 cloves garlic, minced
8 cherry tomatoes, roughly
  chopped
1 pepper (any colour), cut into
  2–3cm pieces
juice of ½ lemon
1 bay leaf
200g paella rice
handful of frozen peas (optional)
3 tbsp parsley, chopped
pepper

SWAP SHOP

1 vegetable stock cube
100g sundried tomatoes
–
1 stick celery, diced
½ tsp garlic powder
1 tbsp tomato puree

100g green beans, cut into
  2–3cm pieces
–
1 tsp dried thyme
200g risotto rice
–
3 tbsp coriander, chopped
–

1. Put on your kettle to boil. Pour 600ml boiling water into a saucepan and stir in the chicken stock cube.

2. Remove the skin from the chorizo and dice it into 2cm cubes.

3. Heat the olive oil in your largest, flattest non-stick frying pan over a medium heat. Add the chorizo and fry for 2 minutes, until almost golden. Move half the chorizo to a plate and leave the oil and the rest of the chorizo in the pan.

4. Fry the onion and garlic together in the oil for 3 minutes before adding in the chopped cherry tomatoes.

5. Add the pepper pieces to the pan along with the lemon juice and bay leaf. Stir-fry for 3 minutes then pour in the paella rice and mix together to coat it in the juices.

6. Pour in 400ml of the chicken stock, cover with a lid or plate and gently simmer for 10 minutes, until the liquid has been absorbed. Don't stir the rice, but give the pan a shake every now and then to stop it sticking.

7. Pour in the remaining 200ml chicken stock, cover with the lid and simmer for 5 minutes.

8. Remove the lid, add a handful of frozen peas, if using, and the rest of the chopped chorizo. Turn the heat up slightly and cook for another 5–7 minutes until all the water has been absorbed.

9. Garnish with the chopped parsley and a pinch of pepper. Serve.

ADDITIONS

50g frozen prawns / 1 tsp chilli flakes lemon wedges, to serve

Swap chorizo for sundried tomatoes to make a delicious veggie variation

BREAKFAST	LUNCH	DINNER	
PINEAPPLE DUTCH BABY PANCAKES WITH CHANTILLY CREAM	CHORIZO, FRIED EGGS AND TOMATOES	THAI GREEN CHICKEN AND COURGETTE CURRY	DAY 1
SAVOURY SUNDRIED TOMATO PORRIDGE	THAI GREEN CURRY RICE CAKES	FETA, CHICKPEA AND COUS COUS SALAD	DAY 2
GRIDDLED PINEAPPLE WITH BUTTER	BIG FAT SPANISH TORTILLA	BEEF NOODLE SALAD IN SATAY SAUCE	DAY 3
EXTRA-CRISPY FRIED EGG ON TOAST	BEEF BANH MI	ROASTED SWEET POTATO, VEG AND FETA	DAY 4
OVERNIGHT VANILLA APPLE OATS	SWEET POTATO MASH WITH BACON AND CARAMELIZED RED ONIONS	THAI BUTTERNUT NOODLES	DAY 5
HASH BROWNS WITH CHORIZO AND EGG	ONE-POT PASTA IN RICH HERBY TOMATO RAGU	CHICKEN AND VEG TAGINE WITH COUS COUS	DAY 6
CHOCOLATE-CHUNK BREAKFAST SCONES	AUBERGINE STACK WITH EGG, BACON AND TOMATO	STUFFED SAVOY CABBAGE	DAY 7

Use leftover curry to make these delicious lunchtime rice cakes

Leftover satay beef makes a tasty baguette

Roast the sweet potato for tomorrow while cooking this

What's in Store?

THIS WEEK'S MEALPLAN begins with a beautiful breakfast sensation – a dreamy Dutch-style pancake filled with Chantilly cream and juicy caramelized pineapple. It follows with a selection of my favourite recipes from the sublime chicken tagine to the mouth-watering Thai Green Curry and Vietnamese Beef Banh Mi.

I recommend freezing portions of the homemade Curry Paste as it will come in handy next time you reach for the takeaway menu! Simply defrost the paste in some boiling coconut milk and cook as usual. You'll have a gorgeous meal quicker than your local can deliver.

If you're in a hurry, the One-pot Pasta is the recipe for you, and if you're after Edinburgh's finest, try the chocolate scones – I've based the recipe on the award-winning version I learnt to make while working there 10 years ago.

Don't forget to read the tips section on pages 10–12 before you go shopping as they'll really help you to save money. As with last week, basic ingredients are not included in the list so make sure you always have chicken, beef or vegetable stock cubes, salt and pepper, caster sugar and olive oil.

Happy cooking!

LUNCH AND DINNER

FRESH PRODUCE

1 aubergine
1 avocado
★ 1 butternut squash
4 carrots
300g cherry tomatoes
2–4 green chillies
125g coriander
3 courgettes
1 cucumber
3 bulbs of garlic
3cm piece of fresh ginger
1 lemon
2 lemongrass stalks
1 lime
★ 1kg onions
4 mixed peppers
2 large potatoes
★ 1kg red onion
180g fresh spinach
1 bunch spring onions
1kg sweet potatoes
★ 2 large tomatoes
★ 1 savoy cabbage

MEAT AND DAIRY

★ 8 rashers of bacon
300g beef steak
★ 250g salted butter
6 chicken thighs, skin-on
and bone-in
★ 200g chorizo
★ 12 free-range eggs
200g feta
250g pork mince
★ 200ml whipping cream

STORE CUPBOARD

1 x 400g tin of chickpeas
1 x 400ml tin of coconut
milk
★ 500g cous cous
★ 18g mixed herbs
★ 345g kalamata olives
★ 500g penne pasta
★ 200g peanuts
★ 500g rice
400g rice noodles
★ 280g sundried tomatoes
★ 92g tikka curry spice
2 x 400g tin of chopped
tomatoes
2 x large (30cm) par-baked
baguettes
85g sage and onion
stuffing

★ Starred ingredients will not be finished this week and
can go towards the breakfast recipes (to supplement the
below), or towards another week.

BREAKFAST

FRESH PRODUCE

2 apples
1 pineapple

MEAT AND DAIRY

12 free-range eggs
500ml whole milk

STORE CUPBOARD

500g self-raising flour
500g oats
100g dark chocolate
35ml vanilla essence

BREAKFAST

LUNCH

Serve with slices of crusty bread for a heartier meal

PINEAPPLE DUTCH BABY PANCAKES WITH CHANTILLY CREAM

SERVES 2 | READY IN 20 MINS | VEGETARIAN

INGREDIENTS

2 eggs
120ml whole milk
pinch of salt
2 tbsp caster sugar
70g self-raising flour
4 tsp vegetable oil
½ pineapple, peeled, core removed and chopped into 2–3cm pieces
1 tsp vanilla essence
100ml whipping cream

SWAP SHOP

–
120ml water
–
1 tbsp honey
70g plain flour
–
4 peaches, chopped into 2–3cm pieces

–
100ml Greek yoghurt

EQUIPMENT

12-hole cupcake tin; or 18–21cm iron skillet, cake tin or ovenproof dish

This recipe makes four mini Dutch pancakes or a large one to share

1. Preheat the oven to 240ºC (fan 220ºC/gas mark 8). Place the cupcake tin or skillet into the oven.

2. Place the eggs into a bowl and add the milk, salt and 1 teaspoon of sugar if you like things sweet. Whisk vigorously until combined, then add the flour and whisk until smooth.

3. For mini pancakes, pour ½ teaspoon of oil each into four of the moulds in the cupcake tin and swirl to coat the sides. For one large pancake, add 1 tablespoon of oil to the skillet. Return to the oven for 2 minutes.

4. Pour in the batter and cook for 5 minutes, then lower the temperature to 200ºC (fan 180ºC/gas mark 6) and cook for another 12–15 minutes, or until the batter rises and is golden.

5. Meanwhile, add the pineapple to a small saucepan along with 1 tablespoon of sugar, 3 tablespoons of water and ½ teaspoon of vanilla. Cook on a medium-low heat for 5 minutes, until the pineapple is glistening and soft.

6. Pour the cream, 1 teaspoon of sugar and ½ teaspoon of vanilla into a bowl. Whisk until thick. Serve the pancake(s) with the pineapple and a spoonful of the whisked Chantilly cream.

ADDITIONS

icing sugar, for dusting / 1 tsp lemon juice

CHORIZO, FRIED EGGS AND TOMATOES

SERVES 2 | READY IN 15 MINS

INGREDIENTS

1 tsp olive oil
1 onion, diced
50g chorizo, sliced into 5mm-thick pieces
6 cherry tomatoes, cut into quarters
2 sundried tomatoes, chopped
4 olives, finely chopped
4 eggs
handful of spinach leaves
pepper

SWAP SHOP

–
–
2 rashers of bacon, sliced into 5mm-thick pieces
½ pepper (any colour), cut into 2–3cm pieces
½ tsp dried mixed herbs
2 artichoke hearts, chopped
–
1 tbsp parsley, chopped
–

1. Heat the oil in a non-stick frying pan over a medium heat. Fry the onion and chorizo for 3 minutes, then add in the cherry tomatoes.

2. Add the sundried tomatoes and olives to the pan. Stir and then make four indents in the ingredients. Crack an egg into each indent and top with the spinach leaves. Lower to a medium-low heat, cover with a lid or plate, and cook for 3–4 minutes, until the egg white has set and the spinach is wilted.

3. Season with black pepper and serve.

ADDITIONS

1 tbsp coriander, chopped / 2 tbsp grated cheddar

DINNER

Save 100ml coconut milk for the satay sauce later this week

THAI GREEN CHICKEN AND COURGETTE CURRY

SERVES 2 | READY IN 30 MINS

COOK ONCE EAT TWICE:
Thai Green Curry Rice Cakes
(Day 2, Lunch, see page 95)

INGREDIENTS

2 tbsp Thai Green
  Curry Paste (see page 160)
4 chicken thighs, bone-in
  and skin-on
salt and pepper
1 x 400ml tin of coconut milk
1 chicken stock cube
1 courgette, cut into
  1cm rounds
1 pepper (any colour), cut
  into 2–3cm pieces
300g rice

SWAP SHOP

–

–

300–400g chicken breast
  or tofu
–
300ml double cream
1 vegetable stock cube
½ aubergine, cut into
  2–3cm fingers
6 mushrooms, cut into
  2–3cm pieces
2 portions of rice noodles
  (about 100g per person)

1. Follow the instructions on page 160 to make a quantity of Thai Green Curry Paste.

2. Using a sharp knife, carefully cut away the fat, skin and bones from the chicken thighs. You can either discard the skin, or season it with salt and pepper and grill it until crisp and serve it on top of the curry.

3. Roughly chop two of the thighs into 3–4cm pieces, and keep the other two thighs whole.

4. Spoon 2 tablespoons of the curry paste into a large saucepan and gently stir-fry for a minute. Add the chicken and stir-fry over a medium heat for 3 minutes, then pour in 300ml coconut milk and 100ml water. Crumble in the stock cube. Stir well, cover and cook for 10 minutes.

5. Put on your kettle to boil. Add the courgette and pepper pieces to the curry pan and gently simmer, uncovered, for 12–15 minutes, or until the vegetables are tender. Meanwhile, add the rice to a saucepan of boiling water and cook for 10–12 minutes.

6. Taste test and season the curry with salt and pepper if necessary. Remove the two whole chicken thighs from the curry, and place on a plate to cool down. Reserve 100g cooked rice and 3 tablespoons of the sauce. You will use these reserved ingredients for tomorrow's Thai Green Curry Rice Cakes (Day 2, Lunch, see page 95).

7. Serve the curry on bowls of steaming rice. Garnish with the chicken skins, if using.

ADDITIONS
1 chilli, de-seeded and finely chopped
1 tbsp coriander, chopped

BREAKFAST

LUNCH

DINNER

SAVOURY SUNDRIED TOMATO PORRIDGE

SERVES 2 | READY IN 10 MINS

INGREDIENTS

100g porridge oats
½ chicken stock cube
1 spring onion, finely chopped

4 sundried tomatoes, diced, plus
  2 extra left whole for garnish
2 eggs
black pepper

SWAP SHOP

–
pinch of salt
3 tbsp chives, finely chopped,
  plus extra for garnish

–

–
–

1. Put on your kettle to boil. Add the porridge oats to a saucepan and pour in 750ml boiling water.

2. Add the stock cube, spring onion and sundried tomatoes, reserving some for a garnish. Bring it all to the boil, then lower the temperature and stir for 8–10 minutes.

3. Meanwhile, re-boil the kettle, add the eggs to a small saucepan and cover with boiling water. Gently simmer for 5 minutes, then remove the eggs and place them in a saucepan or bowl of cold water to halt the cooking process.

4. If the porridge is too thick for your liking, add a small amount of water. When the porridge reaches your desired consistency, divide it between two bowls.

5. Top with a good pinch of black pepper and the extra sundried tomatoes, then peel the eggs and cut them in half. Place on top of each bowl of porridge and tuck in.

ADDITIONS

1 tbsp coriander, chopped
2 rashers of crispy bacon

THAI GREEN CURRY RICE CAKES

SERVES 2 | READY IN 15 MINS
COOK ONCE EAT TWICE:
Thai Green Chicken and Courgette Curry
(Day 1, Dinner, see page 91)

INGREDIENTS	SWAP SHOP
100g leftover cooked rice (see page 91)	–
3 tbsp leftover curry sauce (see page 91)	–
1 tbsp coriander, chopped (optional)	–
salt and pepper	–
1 egg	–
2 tbsp olive oil	–
6–8 savoy cabbage leaves, hard stalk discarded and shredded	250g spring greens, shredded
100g leftover cooked chicken thighs (see page 91)	–

1. Place the leftover cooked rice in a bowl and add the leftover curry sauce and coriander, if using. Season with salt and pepper, crack in the egg and mix well. The rice mixture should be quite wet.

2. Heat 1 tablespoon of the olive oil in a non-stick frying pan over a medium-hot heat. Scoop 1 tablespoon of the rice mixture out of the bowl and shape it into a mini rice cake, about 8cm in diameter and 1cm thick.

3. Place the rice cake in the hot pan and repeat the process until you have used up all of the mixture – you should have 6–8 mini rice cakes in total.

4. Without moving them in the pan, leave the rice cakes to cook for 7 minutes and then carefully turn them over using a spatula. Add the remaining olive oil to the pan and cook the cakes for an additional 5 minutes.

5. Meanwhile, put on your kettle to boil, and fill a large saucepan with boiling water. Plunge the shredded cabbage into the water and simmer for 4–5 minutes, then drain and return to the saucepan.

6. Use two forks to shred the meat from the cooked chicken thighs, then add the meat to the cabbage. Season with salt and pepper and heat through on a low temperature until the cakes are cooked.

7. Pile the cakes onto your plates and top with the chicken and cabbage. Eat hot, or pack them up in airtight containers and take them into work.

ADDITION
chilli sauce

FETA, CHICKPEA AND COUS COUS SALAD

SERVES 2 | READY IN 12 MINS | VEGETARIAN

INGREDIENTS

100g cous cous
½ red onion, very finely sliced
1½ tbsp lemon juice
salt and pepper
1 x 400g tin of chickpeas
1 spring onion, finely chopped
10 olives, chopped
3 tbsp coriander, chopped
handful of spinach leaves,
  shredded
1 pepper (any colour), cut into
  1cm cubes
10cm cucumber, cut into
  1cm cubes
1 avocado, peeled, de-stoned and
  cut into 1cm cubed
2 tbsp olive oil
100g feta

SWAP SHOP

50g rice
½ onion, very finely sliced
1½ tbsp red wine vinegar
–
1 x 400g tin of cannellini beans
3 tbsp chives, chopped
4 sundried tomatoes, chopped
3 tbsp mint, chopped
handful of salad leaves,
  shredded
2 tomatoes, diced

1 stick celery, cut into
  1cm cubes

–

–
100g goat's cheese

1. Put on your kettle to boil.

2. Pour the cous cous into a bowl and pour boiling water over the top until it reaches 1cm above the cous cous. Cover with a plate and leave for 5 minutes.

3. Place the sliced onion in a small bowl with the lemon juice and ½ teaspoon of salt. Mix it together and leave for 5 minutes.

4. Drain and rinse the chickpeas and add them to a large mixing bowl along with the chopped spring onion, olives, coriander and spinach.

5. Add the pepper, cucumber and avocado to the bowl along with the cooked cous cous, and mix everything together.

6. Pour the olive oil on the finely sliced red onion. Mix it together with a fork, then pour it over the salad.

7. Crumble the feta into the salad, toss it all together and season with a pinch of pepper before serving.

ADDITION
½ chilli, de-seeded and finely chopped

Make salads the night before and enjoy tasty packed lunches

LUNCH

BREAKFAST

GRIDDLED PINEAPPLE WITH BUTTER

SERVES 2 | READY IN 10 MINS | VEGETARIAN

INGREDIENTS	SWAP SHOP
1 tbsp butter	–
½ pineapple, peeled, core removed and chopped into quarters	3 peaches, halved
1 tbsp caster sugar	1 tbsp honey or maple syrup
salt and pepper	–

1. Melt the butter in a non-stick griddle or frying pan over a medium-hot heat. Add the pineapple pieces and sprinkle with the sugar. Griddle each side for 2–3 minutes, until caramelized and golden.

2. Remove the pineapple from the heat and lightly season with a little salt and pepper.

3. Slide each piece on a wooden skewer, if available, and eat hot or cold.

ADDITIONS
½ tsp vanilla essence / 2 tbsp Greek yoghurt

BIG FAT SPANISH TORTILLA

SERVES 2 | READY IN 30 MINS

INGREDIENTS	SWAP SHOP
1 large potato, cut into 1cm cubes (about 200g)	4 baby potatoes, cut into 1cm cubes (about 200g)
salt and pepper	–
50g chorizo	2 rashers of bacon
1 tbsp olive oil	–
1 onion, diced	2 cloves garlic, chopped
8 olives, chopped	4 sundried tomatoes, chopped
1 tsp mixed herbs	½ tsp thyme or rosemary
1 pepper (any colour), finely diced	2 tomatoes, finely diced
¼ tsp chilli flakes	½ red chilli, de-seeded and finely chopped
handful of spinach leaves, chopped	3 tbsp coriander, chopped
4 eggs	–
green salad, to serve (optional)	–

1. Put on your kettle to boil.

2. Add the chopped potato to a saucepan of boiling water. Add a pinch of salt and simmer for 10 minutes.

3. Peel the chorizo and discard the skin. Dice it into 1cm cubes.

4. Add 1 teaspoon of olive oil to a non-stick frying pan and fry the chorizo over a medium heat for 1 minute. Add the onion and cook together for 3 minutes before adding the olives, mixed herbs, pepper and chilli flakes.

5. When the potato has cooked, drain it and add to the frying pan along with the chopped spinach. Stir together and arrange the ingredients in an even layer across the pan. Lower the temperature to medium-low.

6. Whisk the eggs in a bowl. Season them with salt and pepper and pour them into the frying pan. Tilt the pan to get an even coverage of egg, then cover with a lid or plate and cook for 5 minutes. Preheat the grill.

7. Remove the lid and place the pan under the grill for 3–5 minutes until it has puffed up and turned golden.

8. Serve it hot or cold, with a simple green salad, if you like.

ADDITIONS
4 cherry tomatoes, halved / chilli sauce

DINNER

BEEF NOODLE SALAD IN SATAY SAUCE

SERVES 2 | READY IN 20 MINS
PLUS MAKING THE PEANUT SATAY SAUCE

COOK ONCE EAT TWICE:
Beef Banh Mi
(Day 4, Lunch, see page 102)

INGREDIENTS

1 quantity Peanut Satay
   Sauce (see page 164)
2 portions of rice noodles (about
   100g per person)
1 large carrot, cut into
   5mm-thick batons
10cm cucumber, cut into
   5mm-thick batons
1 spring onion, finely chopped
3 cherry tomatoes, roughly
   chopped
1 tbsp olive oil
300g beef steak, cut into
   very thin slices
salt and pepper
2 tbsp coriander, chopped
   (optional)

SWAP SHOP

–

2 portions of egg noodles (about
   100g per person)
50g butternut squash, peeled
   and grated
100g radish, sliced into
   5mm pieces
–

¼ pepper (any colour), roughly
   chopped
–

300g chicken or smoked tofu,
   cut into very thin slices
–

–

1. Follow the instructions on page 164 to make a quantity of homemade Peanut Satay Sauce.

2. Put on your kettle to boil. Off the heat, add the rice noodles to a deep saucepan and cover with boiling water. Cover and set aside to cook for 5 minutes.

3. Add the carrot and cucumber batons to a large bowl with the spring onion and the cherry tomatoes.

4. Drain the noodles, refresh them under cold water and then thoroughly drain them again. Add the noodles to the mixing bowl, toss together and divide between two plates, reserving a small handful for tomorrow's lunch (Day 4, Lunch, see page 102).

5. Add the olive oil to a non-stick frying pan over a medium heat. Flash-fry the beef for about 1 minute, until medium-rare. Season with salt and pepper then divide into three portions. Save one portion for tomorrow's lunch (Day 4, Lunch, see page 102), and divide the other two between the plates.

6. Reserving at least 2 tablespoons of the sauce for tomorrow (Day 4, Lunch, see page 102), pour the Satay Sauce over the top and garnish with chopped coriander, if using.

ADDITIONS

small handful of peanuts
2 tbsp mint, chopped
1 chilli, de-seeded and finely sliced

EXTRA-CRISPY FRIED EGG ON TOAST

SERVES 2 | READY IN 15 MINS | VEGETARIAN

INGREDIENTS

1 large par-baked baguette
butter, for spreading
2 tbsp vegetable oil
2 eggs
½ spring onion, finely sliced
salt and pepper

SWAP SHOP

2 slices of crusty toast
–
–
–
4 tbsp chives, finely sliced
–

1. Preheat the oven to 220°C (fan 200°C/gas mark 7). Wet your hands and rub them on the baguette (this will create a nice crust), and bake it in the oven for 8–10 minutes. Cut the baguette in half and butter each slice.

2. Heat a non-stick frying pan until it is extremely hot. Pour 1 tablespoon of vegetable oil into the frying pan, wait for 5–10 seconds until it heats up, then crack in one of the eggs.

3. Sprinkle half of the chopped spring onion onto the egg white and season with salt and pepper.

4. The egg will bubble, begin to puff up, and the edges will turn golden. As soon as the white is set (about 1 minute), remove from the heat and place on the buttered bread. Serve to your significant other, and repeat with the second egg.

ADDITIONS

2cm fresh ginger, grated
1 clove garlic, minced
1 chilli, de-seeded and finely sliced

BEEF BANH MI

SERVES 2 | READY IN 30 MINS

COOK ONCE EAT TWICE:
Beef Noodle Salad in Satay Sauce
(Day 3, Dinner, see page 101)

INGREDIENTS

1 large par-baked baguette
10cm cucumber, cut into
  5mm-thick batons
1 small carrot, cut into
  5mm-thick batons
½ spring onion, finely chopped
small handful leftover rice noodles
  (see page 101)
2 tbsp Peanut Satay
  Sauce (see page 164)
100g leftover cooked beef steak
  (see page 101)
2 tbsp coriander, leaves only

SWAP SHOP

fresh crusty baguette
50g radish, cut into
  5mm pieces
¼ pepper (any colour), cut
  into 5mm-thick batons
3 tbsp chopped chives
1 portion of cooked
  egg noodles
–

100g pan-fried chicken,
  pork or tofu
2 tbsp mint, chopped

1. Preheat the oven to 220°C (fan 200°C/gas mark 7). Wet your hands and rub them on the baguette (this will create a nice crust), and bake it in the oven for 8–10 minutes.

2. Make the mixed salad by adding the cucumber and carrot to a bowl with the chopped spring onion and the leftover rice noodles.

3. Slice the baguette in half along the length and spread it with the Peanut Satay Sauce. Top with the mixed salad, rice noodles and cooked beef steak.

4. Garnish with the coriander, then cut it into two 15cm subs and enjoy. You can also wrap it in foil and take it to work.

ADDITIONS

½ onion, sliced thinly and fried / chilli sauce
1 chilli, de-seeded and finely sliced

BREAKFAST

LUNCH

DINNER

Save time tomorrow, make the Sweet Potato Mash today (see page 108)

ROASTED SWEET POTATO, VEG AND FETA

SERVES 2 | READY IN 20 MINS | VEGETARIAN

COOK ONCE EAT TWICE:
Sweet Potato Mash with Bacon and Caramelized Red Onions (Day 5, Lunch, see page 108)

INGREDIENTS

1kg sweet potatoes, skin-on and halved

1½ tbsp olive oil, plus extra for drizzling

3 cloves garlic, minced

8 olives, chopped

1 tsp mixed herbs

salt and pepper

8 cherry tomatoes

1 pepper (any colour), roughly chopped

1 courgette, cut into 2cm-thick slices

2 red onions, each cut into 8 wedges

50g feta

SWAP SHOP

500g butternut squash, seeds removed and cut into quarters

–

–

4 sundried tomatoes, chopped

1 tsp dried thyme, basil or rosemary

–

½ tin of chopped tomatoes

6 mushrooms, roughly chopped

½ broccoli, cut into 2cm-thick slices

2 onions, each cut into 8 wedges

50g goat's cheese

1. Preheat the oven to 200°C (fan 180°C/gas mark 6).

2. Place half the sweet potato in a large oven tray. Add the other half to a smaller roasting tray, drizzle with olive oil and set aside.

3. Make the marinade by placing the garlic in a bowl along with the chopped olives, mixed herbs, 1½ tablespoons of olive oil and a good pinch of salt and pepper.

4. Cut the cherry tomatoes in half and squeeze the juice and pips into the marinade bowl, then place the tomato skins in the oven tray.

5. Add the pepper and courgette to the large tray along with red onion wedges.

6. Stir the marinade and pour it over the vegetables in the large tray. Toss together so that all of the vegetables are coated.

7. Transfer both trays to the middle shelf in the oven and bake for 40 minutes, until the vegetables are soft.

8. Crumble the feta over the vegetables in the larger oven tray and serve. Set aside the smaller tray of roasted sweet potato for making tomorrow's lunch (Day 5, Lunch, see page 108).

LUNCH

BREAKFAST

DINNER

OVERNIGHT VANILLA APPLE OATS

SERVES 2 | READY IN 10 MINS | VEGETARIAN

INGREDIENTS

2 apples
100g porridge oats
100ml whole milk
1 tsp vanilla essence (optional)
2 tbsp whipping cream

SWAP SHOP

1 ripe pear
–
100ml apple juice
–
2 tbsp yoghurt

Make the night before and eat in the morning

1. Leaving the skin on, grate the apples and divide them between two bowls.

2. Add 50g of the porridge oats to each bowl and pour 50ml of the milk over the top.

3. Add ½ teaspoon of vanilla essence to each bowl, if using, then stir everything together and place both bowls in the fridge.

4. In the morning, mix 1 tablespoon of the cream into each bowl. Enjoy!

ADDITIONS

2 tsp honey / handful of nuts
small handful of blueberries

SWEET POTATO MASH WITH BACON AND CARAMELIZED RED ONIONS

SERVES 2 | READY IN 15 MINS

INGREDIENTS

6 small or 4 medium red onions
salt and pepper
1 tbsp olive oil
4 rashers of bacon
1 tbsp butter
500g roasted sweet potato pieces
  (see page 105)

SWAP SHOP

8 shallots
–
–
2 sausages
1 tbsp olive oil
500g baked potatoes

1. Put on your kettle to boil and preheat the oven to 200°C (fan 180°C/gas mark 6).

2. Cut the top and bottom off the red onions and peel them whole. Add them to a saucepan and cover with boiling water. Add a pinch of salt and gently simmer for 8–10 minutes, then drain and place the onions back in the pan.

3. Add the butter along with a good pinch of salt. Stir together until the butter has melted and coats the onions. Transfer to an oven dish and stand them upright on their bottoms. Bake in the oven for 25–30 minutes.

4. Meanwhile, add the olive oil to a non-stick frying pan and cook the bacon until crisp. Heat the roasted sweet potatoes in the microwave until hot.

5. Take the warmed sweet potatoes and gently mash them with a fork. Add the roasted onions and top with the crispy bacon.

6. Eat immediately or pack it up for lunch – it can be re-heated in a microwave.

ADDITIONS

beef gravy, to serve / 1 tsp thyme

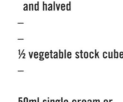

You only need half of the squash to make this. Keep the other unpeeled half in the fridge for 4–5 days

THAI BUTTERNUT NOODLES

SERVES 2 | READY IN 35 MINS

INGREDIENTS

500g butternut squash (about
½ small one), peeled and halved
1 tbsp olive oil
salt and pepper
½ chicken stock cube
1 tbsp Thai Green
Curry Paste (see page 160)
50ml whipping cream

2 portions of rice noodles (about
100g per person)

EQUIPMENT
stick blender

SWAP SHOP

500g sweet potatoes, skin-on
and halved
–
–
½ vegetable stock cube
–

50ml single cream or
coconut milk
2 portions of egg noodles
(about 100g per person)

1. Put on your kettle to boil and preheat the oven to 200°C (fan 180°C/gas mark 6).

2. Chop one of the butternut squash pieces into six slices. Add the slices to an oven tray, toss in the olive oil and season with salt and pepper. Bake for 15–20 minutes until soft.

3. Cut the other piece into 1–2cm cubes and add to a small saucepan along with the stock cube, Thai Green Curry Paste and 200ml boiling water.

4. Allow to boil for 10 minutes until soft then use a stick blender to blitz to a thick soup-like consistency. Stir the cream into the sauce and keep warm until you're ready to serve.

5. Put on your kettle to boil. Off the heat, add the noodles to a deep saucepan and cover with boiling water. Cover and set aside to cook for 5 minutes.

6. Pour the sauce into two bowls, drain the noodles and add a portion to each bowl, then top with the roasted squash and garnish with coriander, if you like.

ADDITIONS
1 chilli, de-seeded and finely sliced
1 tbsp coriander, chopped

HASH BROWNS WITH CHORIZO AND EGG

SERVES 2 | READY IN 15 MINS

INGREDIENTS

300g potato (about 1 large one), grated
salt and pepper
3 eggs
50g chorizo
1 tbsp olive oil

SWAP SHOP

300g sweet potatoes, grated
–
–
2 rashers of bacon
–

1. Squeeze a handful of grated potato over the sink to remove excess water, then transfer to a bowl. Repeat with the remaining potato, then season generously. Stir through one of the eggs.

2. Peel the chorizo and discard the skin. Slice the meat into 5mm-thick pieces.

3. Heat the olive oil in a non-stick frying pan over a medium-hot heat. Scoop 1 tablespoon of the potato mixture out of the bowl and shape it into a pattie, about 8cm in diameter and 1cm thick. Place it in the pan and repeat the process with the remaining mixture – you should get 6–8 hash browns in total.

4. Fry the hash browns for 5–6 minutes, then flip them over with a spatula and fry for 5 minutes. Add the chorizo to the pan for the last 5 minutes, turning once after 2½ minutes.

5. Meanwhile, put on your kettle to boil. Add the remaining eggs to a saucepan and cover with boiling water. Gently simmer for 5 minutes, then run them under cool water for 30 seconds.

6. Divide the hash browns and chorizo between two plates. Roll the eggs on a table to crack the shells, then peel and serve on top.

ONE-POT PASTA IN RICH HERBY TOMATO RAGU

SERVES 2 | READY IN 20 MINS

INGREDIENTS

1 chicken stock cube
3 tsp mixed herbs

¼ tsp chilli flakes

1 x 400g tin of chopped tomatoes
150g penne pasta
1 onion, finely sliced
2 cloves garlic, minced
4–6 sundried tomatoes, roughly chopped
50g feta, crumbled
salt and pepper

SWAP SHOP

1 vegetable stock cube
3 tsp dried thyme, rosemary or basil
½ chilli, de-seeded and finely chopped
–
2 portions of spaghetti
–
–
10 olives, roughly chopped

50g cheddar, grated
–

1. Put on your kettle to boil.

2. Add 300ml boiling water to a deep saucepan and crumble in the chicken stock cube. Add the mixed herbs, chilli flakes and chopped tomatoes.

3. Add the pasta, onion, garlic and sundried tomatoes, then stir together.

4. Place a lid on the saucepan and boil over a medium-high heat for 10 minutes. Remove the lid and continue to boil for another 7 minutes, stirring occasionally.

5. Stir the feta through the hot pasta. Taste test, season with salt and pepper if needed, and serve.

ADDITIONS
small handful of basil

If you don't have feta, try crumbled goat's cheese or grated cheddar

LUNCH

BREAKFAST

DINNER

CHICKEN AND VEG TAGINE WITH COUS COUS

SERVES 2 | READY IN 1 HR 15 MINS

INGREDIENTS

1 onion, cut into half-moon slices
2 cloves garlic, minced
2 tbsp olive oil
1 tsp mixed herbs

2 tsp tikka spice
2 chicken thighs, bone-in and
  skin-on
2 carrots, roughly chopped into
  3–4cm pieces
1 courgette, roughly chopped
  into 3–4cm pieces
2 chicken stock cubes
200g cous cous

SWAP SHOP

–
–
–

½ tsp dried thyme, oregano
  or rosemary
2 tsp tandoori spice
2 chicken legs, bone-in and
  skin-on
2 potatoes, roughly chopped into
  3–4cm pieces
½ aubergine, roughly chopped
  into 3–4cm pieces
2 vegetable stock cubes
150g rice

> Get your hands on preserved lemons, or lime pickle, and add a chopped teaspoon to the finished dish

1. Put on your kettle to boil.

2. Add the onion and garlic to a deep saucepan along with the oil. Fry over a medium heat for 3–4 minutes.

3. Add the mixed herbs, tikka spice and chicken thighs, skin-side down. Cook for a further 4–5 minutes, stirring occasionally.

4. Add the carrots and courgette to the saucepan along with 1 crumbled chicken stock cube and enough boiling water to just cover the chicken. Stir together, bring to the boil and put a lid on top. Lower the temperature to a low simmer and cook for a total of 1 hour (flipping the chicken after 30 minutes and carefully removing the skin).

5. Check the water levels and stir occasionally to stop it from sticking to the bottom of the saucepan. The tagine should be moist with a little juice. If there is too much water, turn up the heat and cook off some of the liquid.

6. Around 10 minutes before serving, make the cous cous. Pour the cous cous into a bowl and crumble in the remaining chicken stock cube and a good pinch of pepper. Stir, then pour boiling water over the top until it reaches 1cm above the cous cous. Cover with a plate and leave for 6–8 minutes.

7. Divide the cous cous between two plates and top with the chicken tagine.

ADDITIONS
2 tbsp coriander, chopped / ½ tsp cinnamon
1 chilli, de-seeded and finely sliced

LUNCH

BREAKFAST

DINNER

Check if the scones are cooked by tapping one on the base. It should sound slightly hollow

CHOCOLATE-CHUNK BREAKFAST SCONES

SERVES 2 | READY IN 25 MINS

INGREDIENTS	SWAP SHOP
250g self-raising flour, plus extra for dusting	–
50g dark chocolate, chopped into 1cm chunks	50g raisins
50g caster sugar	–
pinch of salt	–
50g butter	50g margarine
100ml whole milk	–
50ml whipping cream	50ml whole milk

1. Preheat the oven to 200°C (fan 180°C/gas mark 6).

2. Add the flour, chopped dark chocolate, sugar and salt to a mixing bowl.

3. Melt the butter in a small saucepan over a low heat. Take it off the heat and mix in the milk and cream. Stir together, then pour it into the dry ingredients.

4. Use a spoon to bring the ingredients together, and once combined, tip out the mixture onto a clean, lightly floured surface.

5. Use your hands to knead the dough together for 1 minute until soft. If it is too sticky, add small amounts of flour.

6. Divide the dough into four pieces and shape each one into a scone shape, about 6cm in diameter and 4cm thick. Place on a lightly floured baking tray and dust the tops with a small amount of flour.

7. Bake the scones in the middle of the oven for 18–20 minutes until golden. Cool them on a wire rack for a few minutes before serving with your morning coffee.

To serve with chicken skin, save the skin from two chicken thighs. Grill for 10–15 minutes and add to the stack at step 5

AUBERGINE STACK WITH EGG, BACON AND TOMATO

SERVES 2 | READY IN 30 MINS

INGREDIENTS

1 aubergine, cut into 5mm-thick slices
salt and pepper
1½ tbsp olive oil
½ clove garlic, minced
2 large tomatoes, sliced
4 rashers of bacon
2 eggs
½ spring onion, finely chopped

SWAP SHOP

2 courgettes, cut into 5mm-thick slices
–
–
–
6 cherry tomatoes, halved
4 crispy chicken-thigh skins
–
–

1. Place the aubergine in a bowl with a good pinch of salt and pepper, 1 tablespoon of the olive oil and the garlic. Use your hands to mix and toss the ingredients together.

2. Place the tomato and aubergine slices on a tray and grill on high heat for 3–5 minutes each side or until they start to brown. Keep an eye on them as they can burn easily.

3. At the same time, heat 1 teaspoon of olive oil in a non-stick frying pan over a medium heat. Add the bacon and begin to cook.

4. Move the bacon to one side of the frying pan and crack the eggs into the pan. Sprinkle the egg white with the spring onion, along with a pinch of pepper.

5. The bacon, aubergine and egg should all finish cooking at roughly the same time. Stack onto two plates and enjoy.

ADDITIONS
small handful of basil leaves / crusty bread

STUFFED SAVOY CABBAGE

SERVES 2 | READY IN 45 MINS

INGREDIENTS

1 x 85g packet sage and
  onion stuffing
8–10 large savoy cabbage leaves,
  washed
1 x 400g tin of chopped tomatoes
salt and pepper
2 cloves garlic, minced
1 bay leaf
250g pork mince

EQUIPMENT

18–21cm ovenproof dish

SWAP SHOP

–

8–10 Chinese cabbage leaves,
  washed
–
–
–
–
200g sausage meat

1. Put on your kettle to boil and preheat the oven to 200°C (fan 180°C/gas mark 6).

2. Tip the sage and onion stuffing into a bowl and pour 200ml boiling water over the top. Cover with a plate and leave to expand.

3. Place the savoy cabbage leaves in a large saucepan and cover with boiling water. Gently simmer for 5 minutes until soft, then drain and refresh under cold running water for 10 seconds. Set aside and allow to dry.

4. Pour the chopped tomatoes into a small saucepan. Add a good pinch of salt, the garlic and the bay leaf. Bring to the boil, then place a lid on the pan and turn off the heat.

5. Take each cabbage leaf and slice either side of the hard stem, from the thick base all the way to 3–4cm from the top. Cut out the stem, leaving the top attached.

6. Pour most of the tomato sauce into the oven dish. Add the pork mince to the sage and onion stuffing and mix well.

7. Lay out a cabbage leaf on the work surface and slightly overlap the leaf where the stem used to be. Mix the stuffing, then take a golf-ball-sized piece and and roll it into a small sausage using your hands. Place it on the centre of the leaf, bring the sides of the leaf in and then roll it up like a fat cigar.

8. Repeat the process with the remaining leaves and place each one in the ovenproof dish with the tomato sauce.

9. Spoon the remaining sauce over the top and bake in the middle of the oven for 30 minutes. Season with pepper and serve hot.

ADDITION
50g raisins

Make a double batch of the stuffing and freeze half in small balls. Defrost and cook in the oven for 20–25 minutes

WEEK
4
Mealplan

BREAKFAST	LUNCH	DINNER	
SPROUTS AND BACON WITH BOILED EGGS	PESTO PANCAKES WITH MUSHROOMS	HEARTY BEEF STEW	DAY 1
CHOCOLATE AND BANANA PANCAKES	MANGO, BLACK BEAN AND RICE SALAD	PAN-FRIED PORK AND HALLOUMI SPAGHETTI	DAY 2
GRILLED PEACHES WITH YOGHURT	SAUSAGE AND BABY POTATO TRAY BAKE	MELT-IN-THE-MOUTH BEAN BURGERS WITH SWEET POTATO FRIES	DAY 3
HONEY-ROASTED SPROUTS WITH HUMMUS ON TOAST	KOFTA MASALA CURRY	HERBY ROAST VEGETABLE RISOTTO	DAY 4
PEACH CLAFOUTIS WITH GREEK YOGHURT	PARMESAN BREADCRUMB RISOTTO CAKES	GNOCCHI WITH SPINACH AND PESTO	DAY 5
CHOCOLATE-DIPPED FRUIT	LENTIL SALAD WITH HALLOUMI, MUSHROOMS AND SPINACH	ROAST ROOT VEGETABLE TRAY BAKE	DAY 6
ENGLISH BREAKFAST IN A YORKSHIRE	COUNTRY VEG SOUP	BEEF IN FIVE SPICE	DAY 7

Double up on batter to make tomorrow's breakfast pancakes

These use up leftovers from yesterday's risotto

Blitz up leftovers from the tray bake to make soup

What's in Store?

THIS WEEK'S MEALPLAN is a combination of ultra-quick recipes and longer, slow-cooked wonders that make full use of the oven. I'll show you how simple it is to prep ingredients and let the oven do its thing, leaving you with more leisure time to enjoy. You'll be rewarded with hearty potato and sausage tray bakes, light summer risottos and rich beef stews, as well as a selection of 15–20-minute meals such as the summery lentil and halloumi salad and chocolate pancakes.

The homemade Pesto (see page 158) doubles up as a fantastic dip for nachos as well as providing intense flavour for the gnocchi. It's my take on the Italian classic but gives a richer, creamier experience due to the addition of cream cheese. I think you'll love it!

Don't forget to read the tips section on pages 10–12 before you go shopping as they'll really help you to save money. As with last week, basic ingredients are not included in the list so make sure you always have chicken, beef or vegetable stock cubes, salt and pepper, caster sugar and olive oil.

Happy cooking!

LUNCH AND DINNER

FRESH PRODUCE

1.5kg baby potatoes

25g basil

★ 1kg carrots

600g cherry tomatoes

60g red chillies

1 courgette

80g coriander

180g spinach leaves

4 bulbs of garlic

6cm piece of fresh ginger

1 lime

★ 1 lemon

1 mango

800g mushrooms

★ 1kg onions

500g parsnips

★ 3 peppers (mixed colours)

★ 1kg red onion

1 bunch of spring onions

1 sweet potato

★ 5 large tomatos

2 turnips

MEAT AND DAIRY

beef brisket (700–1kg)

★ 250g butter

★ 250g cream cheese

★ 6 free-range eggs

250g halloumi cheese

★ 2 pints whole milk

160g parmesan

6 sausages

STORE CUPBOARD

1 x 400g tin of black beans

2 x 400g tins of black-eyed beans

★ 800g bread

2 burger buns

1 x 400g tin of chickpeas

★ 30g Chinese five spice

1 x 400g tin of lentils

500g gnocchi

★ 18g mixed herbs

★ 500g plain flour

★ 1kg rice

★ 500g risotto rice

★ 500g spaghetti

★ 100g tikka spice

2 x 400g tins of chopped tomatoes

★ Starred ingredients will not be finished this week and can go towards the breakfast recipes (to supplement the below), or towards another week.

BREAKFAST

FRESH PRODUCE

4 bananas

1 courgette

1 lemon

500g brussels sprouts

6 peaches

2 oranges

MEAT AND DAIRY

8 rashers of bacon

12 free-range eggs

500g Greek yoghurt

STORE CUPBOARD

1 x 400g tin of chickpeas

150g dark chocolate

300ml honey

LUNCH

BREAKFAST

SPROUTS AND BACON WITH BOILED EGGS

SERVES 2 | READY IN 15 MINS

INGREDIENTS	SWAP SHOP
250g brussels sprouts	250g savoy cabbage
½ tbsp butter	–
4 rashers of bacon, cut into 1–2cm pieces	4 sundried tomatoes, cut into 1–2cm pieces
2 eggs	–
salt and pepper	–
toast (optional)	–

1. Wash the sprouts and remove discoloured outer leaves. Chop 5mm from each base to create a flat surface. Rest each sprout on its flat bottom and slice it into four pieces.

2. Melt the butter in a non-stick frying pan over a medium-hot heat. Add the sprouts and bacon and mix together. Place a lid or large plate over the frying pan, turn the heat to medium-low and cook for 10 minutes, stirring occasionally to stop any sticking. Put on your kettle to boil.

3. After 5 minutes of cooking, pour the boiling water into a saucepan, bring to a simmer and slide in the eggs. Cook for 5½ minutes, then cool them under cold running water.

4. Peel and halve the eggs. Season the mixture in the pan with salt and pepper, divide it between two bowls and top with the eggs and toast, if you like.

ADDITIONS
1 tbsp grated parmesan / chilli sauce

PESTO PANCAKES WITH MUSHROOMS

SERVES 2 | READY IN 20 MINS
PLUS MAKING THE PESTO

INGREDIENTS	SWAP SHOP
2 tbsp Pesto (see page 158)	–
150ml whole milk	150ml water
1 egg	–
salt and pepper	–
50g plain flour	50g self-raising flour
250g mushrooms, cut into quarters	1–2 courgettes, cut into 2–3cm pieces
1 tbsp butter	1 tsp olive oil
handful of spinach leaves	handful of rocket

Double the batter quantity and divide into two portions. Keep one portion in the fridge for tomorrow (see page 130)

1. Follow the instructions on page 158 to make a quantity of Pesto.

2. Make the pancake batter by whisking together the milk, egg, a pinch of salt and the flour until a smooth batter has formed.

3. Place the mushrooms in a hot frying pan with 1 teaspoon butter. Stir-fry for 2–3 minutes until they are hot through but still firm. Season, then add the spinach and cook for 30 seconds until wilted.

4. Melt 1 teaspoon of the butter in a large, non-stick frying pan over a medium heat. Pour in half the batter, or enough to thinly coat the surface of the pan. Tilt and rotate the pan.

5. Cook for about 2 minutes, until firm, then flip over with a spatula and cook for 1 minute.

6. Spread 1 tablespoon of Pesto on the pancake and top with half the mushroom mixture. Serve and make another one.

ADDITION
100g cooked chicken, shredded

HEARTY BEEF STEW

SERVES 2 | READY IN 3 HRS 20 MINS

INGREDIENTS

350–500g beef brisket
salt and pepper
2 tbsp olive oil
2 onions, sliced
4 cloves garlic, minced
4 large tomatoes, roughly chopped
1 beef stock cube
1 bay leaf (optional)
1 tsp mixed herbs
1 tbsp plain flour
350g baby potatoes

2 carrots, chopped into
  5cm pieces
100g mushrooms, left whole

SWAP SHOP

350–500g beef roasting joint
—
2 tbsp butter
2 sticks celery, sliced
½ tsp garlic powder
2 tbsp tomato puree
1 chicken stock cube
—
1 tsp rosemary or thyme
1 tbsp cornflour
350g potatoes, chopped
  into 5cm pieces
2 beetroots, chopped into
  5cm pieces
1 courgette, chopped into
  5cm pieces

1. Put on your kettle to boil.

2. Trim the beef of any excess fat and cut the meat into 4cm chunks. Generously season with pepper.

3. Add 1 tablespoon of the oil to a large saucepan over a medium heat. Add half the meat and brown it for 5–6 minutes, turning occasionally until all sides are browned – you're looking for a good crust. Transfer the meat to a plate and repeat the process with the second batch. Leave on the plate to rest.

4. Add the onion and garlic to the saucepan along with the tomatoes, 3 tablespoons of water and a good pinch of salt. Use a wooden spoon to scrape the brown bits from the pan, stirring for 3 minutes to soften the onions.

5. Add the beef back to the pan with the meat juices, stock cube, bay leaf (if using), mixed herbs and flour and just cover with boiling water. Bring to the boil, place a lid on the saucepan and reduce the temperature to a bubbling simmer for 2 hours.

6. After 2 hours, add the baby potatoes, carrots and the mushrooms, left whole. Top up the water to cover the potatoes, then simmer without a lid for another hour, stirring occasionally, until the sauce is thick and the meat is tender.

7. Taste test and season with salt and pepper as necessary. If there is too much liquid, turn the heat up and cook off the excess. Divide between two bowls and serve.

ADDITIONS

125ml red wine / 1 red chilli, left whole

DINNER

BREAKFAST

LUNCH

DINNER

CHOCOLATE AND BANANA PANCAKES

SERVES 2 | READY IN 20 MINS | VEGETARIAN

INGREDIENTS

50g dark chocolate, plus extra
  for grating (optional)
1 tbsp caster sugar (optional)
150ml whole milk
1 egg
pinch of salt
65g plain flour
1 tbsp butter, plus 2 tsp
2 ripe bananas
1 tbsp honey
2 tbsp Greek yoghurt

SWAP SHOP

50g any chocolate, plus extra
  for grating (optional)
–
150ml water
–
–
65g self-raising flour
3 tsp olive oil
¼ pineapple
2 tsp caster sugar
2 tbsp yoghurt

1. Roughly chop the chocolate and place it in a small pan with 3 tablespoons of water and the sugar, if using. Gently heat until the chocolate has melted, then remove from the heat, quickly whisk together to combine and leave to cool.

2. If you didn't make double quantities yesterday, make the batter by whisking together the milk, egg, salt and flour. Whisk thoroughly until a smooth batter has formed, then pour it into the melted chocolate and whisk to combine. Leave the batter to rest while you prepare the banana.

3. Melt 1 tablespoon of the butter in a non-stick frying pan over a medium heat. Peel the bananas and cut them in half lengthways. Add the bananas to the frying pan and cook for 5 minutes before flipping them over. Drizzle over the honey, turn the heat to low and keep them warm until the pancakes are cooked.

4. When you have flipped the bananas over, make the pancakes. Melt 1 teaspoon of the butter in a large, non-stick frying pan over a medium heat. Pour in half the batter, or enough to thinly coat the surface of the frying pan. Tilt and rotate the pan for even coverage.

5. Cook for around 2 minutes until firm, then flip with a spatula and cook for 1 minute.

6. Serve immediately with 1 tablespoon of Greek yoghurt, one caramelized banana and some grated chocolate, if you like. Serve and make another one.

ADDITION
1 tsp vanilla essence

MANGO, BLACK BEAN AND RICE SALAD

SERVES 2 | READY IN 15 MINS | VEGETARIAN

INGREDIENTS

100g rice
1 x 400g tin of black beans
1 ripe mango, peeled, de-stoned
  and cut into 1cm pieces
1 pepper (any colour), cut
  into 1cm pieces
150g cherry tomatoes, cut into
  1cm pieces
2 spring onions, finely chopped
½ red chilli, de-seeded
  and finely chopped
¼ clove garlic, crushed to a paste
2 tbsp coriander, chopped
juice of 1 lime
salt and pepper
2 tbsp olive oil

SWAP SHOP

100g cous cous
1 x 400g tin of black-eyed beans
½ pineapple, peeled, cored
  and cut into 1cm pieces
1 carrot, cut into 1cm pieces

150g chopped tomatoes

¼ red onion, finely chopped
½ tsp chilli flakes

–
2 tbsp parsley, chopped
juice of 1 lemon
–
–

1. Put on your kettle to boil.

2. Place the rice in a saucepan and fill with salted boiling water. Cook for 10–12 minutes until done, then drain and rinse under cold water. Drain thoroughly and leave to cool while you prepare the salad.

3. Drain and rinse the black beans under cold running water, drain well and then place them in a large bowl.

4. Add the mango, pepper and tomato cubes to the bowl, followed by the spring onions, chilli, garlic, coriander and lime juice.

5. Add the cooled rice, season well with salt and pepper and stir through the olive oil. Mix it all together and enjoy.

ADDITION
handful of nachos

Before you juice a lime, roll it on a surface for 30 seconds. This breaks down the membrane so you can squeeze more juice

PAN-FRIED PORK AND HALLOUMI SPAGHETTI

SERVES 2 | READY IN 35 MINS

INGREDIENTS

1 tbsp olive oil, plus 1 tsp
4 red onions, cut into 8 segments
2 cloves garlic, sliced
3 sausages

salt and pepper
2 portions of spaghetti (about 100g per person)
125g halloumi cheese

SWAP SHOP

1 tbsp butter, plus 1 tsp
4 onions, cut into 8 segments
–
3 veggie sausages (I use Cauldron's)
–
2 portions of rice (about 50g per person)
125g feta

1. Heat 1 tablespoon of the olive oil in a non-stick frying pan over a medium heat. Throw in the onion and garlic and lower to a medium-low heat.

2. Cut the sausages into 1cm pieces and add them to the frying pan. Stir, season with salt and pepper and leave them to brown for 15 minutes.

3. Meanwhile, put on your kettle to boil. Pour the boiling water into a medium saucepan, add a pinch of salt and cook the spaghetti for 10–12 minutes.

4. When the spaghetti is cooked, drain it and return to the saucepan. Add the onion and sausage meat, stir together and place a lid on the saucepan to keep it hot.

5. Cut the halloumi into 5mm-thick slices, then tear it into 2–3cm widths. Add it to the frying pan along with 1 teaspoon of oil. Fry over a medium heat for 1–2 minutes, until the underside is golden, then turn them all over and fry for another minute.

6. Add the halloumi to the spaghetti, season with black pepper and serve hot.

ADDITIONS
handful of sage leaves, fried
1 tbsp grated parmesan

Mix up your meat with big flavours, such as halloumi or sundried tomatoes, and you can make it go so much further

BREAKFAST

LUNCH

DINNER

GRILLED PEACHES WITH YOGHURT

SERVES 2 | READY IN 5 MINS

INGREDIENTS

3 ripe peaches, halved and
 de-stoned
2 tbsp honey
2 tbsp Greek yoghurt

SWAP SHOP

4 grapefruit halves,
 unpeeled
1 tbsp maple syrup
2 tbsp crème fraiche

Plums and apricots are also delicious grilled

1. Turn the grill on to a hot heat. If you don't have a grill, these can also be cooked in a non-stick frying pan or griddle over a medium-hot heat.

2. Place the peach halves on a baking tray, skin-side down. Drizzle the honey over the flesh and place the peaches under the grill for 5 minutes.

3. Serve hot with Greek yoghurt.

ADDITIONS

nuts and seeds, to serve
handful of sage leaves, fried

SAUSAGE AND BABY POTATO TRAY BAKE

SERVES 2 | READY IN 45 MINS

INGREDIENTS
500g baby potatoes
salt and pepper
3 sausages

2 red onions, each cut into
  8 segments
1 pepper (any colour), cut into
  4–5cm pieces
1 tbsp olive oil
1 tsp butter
2 cloves garlic, minced

SWAP SHOP
500g potatoes, chopped
—

3 vegetarian sausages, or
  2 chicken thighs, bone-in
2 onions, each cut into
  8 segments
1 courgette, cut into
  4–5cm pieces
—
—
1 tsp mixed herbs

If you decide to use chicken thighs instead of sausages, increase the oven time to 45 minutes

1. Put on your kettle to boil and preheat the oven to 200°C (fan 180°C/gas mark 6).

2. If any of the potatoes are large in size, cut them in half so that they cook evenly. Add the potatoes to a large saucepan and fill it with boiling water. Add a pinch of salt and simmer for 10 minutes.

3. Cut the sausages into three pieces. Add the chopped red onions, pepper and sausage pieces to a large oven tray and pour over the olive oil and a good pinch of salt and pepper. Shake together to coat the vegetables.

4. When the potatoes are cooked, drain well and return them to the saucepan along with the butter and garlic. Season with salt and pepper.

5. Vigorously shake the potatoes to coat them in the garlic butter, then transfer them to the oven tray.

6. Roast the tray bake in the middle of the oven for 30 minutes. Serve.

ADDITION
2 large tomatoes, left whole

MELT-IN-THE-MOUTH BEAN BURGERS WITH SWEET POTATO FRIES

SERVES 2 | READY IN 35 MINS | VEGETARIAN

COOK ONCE EAT TWICE:
Kofta Masala Curry
(Day 4, Lunch, see page 141)

INGREDIENTS

2 x 400g tins of black-eyed beans
1 small onion, grated
1 clove garlic, grated
2½ tsp tikka spice
2 tsp flour
salt and pepper
1 tbsp olive oil
2 burger buns

For the sweet potato fries

1 large sweet potato, cut into
   long 1cm-thick chips
2 tsp olive oil
1 tsp flour
salt
1 tsp mixed herbs (optional)

SWAP SHOP

2 x 400g tins of kidney beans
4 spring onions, grated
¼ tsp garlic powder
2½ tsp tandoori spice
1 tbsp breadcrumbs
–
–
2 ciabatta rolls

1 large potato, cut into long
   1cm-thick chips
–
–
–
–

1. To make the sweet potato fries, turn on the grill to a medium heat. Place the sweet potato chips in a baking tray and add the olive oil. Toss to coat the fries in the oil, and then add the flour, a good pinch of salt and the mixed herbs, if using.

2. Toss again to coat the fries, then place them under the grill for 30–35 minutes, until golden and crisp, turning midway through the cooking time. Don't overcrowd the tray or they will not crisp up.

3. Meanwhile, rinse the beans under running water. Shake them very well to dry and transfer to a bowl. Add the onion, garlic, tikka spice, flour and a pinch of salt and pepper.

4. Thoroughly mix and mash the ingredients together using clean hands to make a rough paste from the beans.

5. Heat the oil in a non-stick frying pan over a medium-hot heat. Form the burger mix into four equal patties. Set two burgers aside for tomorrow's lunch: Kofta Masala Curry (Day 4, Lunch, see page 141). You can also freeze the burgers for up to 3 months.

6. Fry the other two burgers for 3–4 minutes on one side, then flip them over to cook on the other side for another 3–4 minutes.

7. Toast the bread roll, layer with the fillings of your choice and enjoy your masterpiece.

ADDITIONS

2 tsp mayo or ketchup / 1 tomato, sliced
lettuce leaves / ½ avocado, de-stoned and sliced
1 tbsp grated cheddar / 2 fried eggs / hot sauce
2 rashers of crispy bacon

If you don't have a grater, chop the onion and garlic very finely and fry in oil for 3 minutes

LUNCH

BREAKFAST

HONEY-ROASTED SPROUTS WITH HUMMUS ON TOAST

SERVES 2 | READY IN 20 MINS
PLUS MAKING THE NAANS | VEGETARIAN

INGREDIENTS	SWAP SHOP
250g brussels sprouts, cut into quarters	250g cauliflower florets
1 tbsp butter, chopped	–
salt and pepper	–
4 tbsp Hummus (see page 158)	–
1 heaped tsp honey	1 heaped tsp maple syrup
2 slices of toast	2 plain tortilla wraps
½ tsp chilli flakes (optional)	½ tsp chilli sauce (optional)

1. Preheat the oven to 200ºC (fan 180ºC/gas mark 6). Place an oven dish inside to heat as the oven preheats.

2. When the oven is hot, place the sprouts in the oven dish along with the butter. Season with salt and pepper and roast for 10 minutes.

3. Meanwhile, follow the instructions on page 158 to make a quantity of Hummus.

4. Dollop the honey on top of the roasted sprouts and toss together. Return to the oven and roast for 5 minutes.

5. Generously spread the toast with Hummus and top with the honey-roasted sprouts. Finish with a pinch of chilli flakes, if you like.

KOFTA MASALA CURRY

SERVES 2 | READY IN 15 MINS
PLUS MAKING THE NAANS
COOK ONCE EAT TWICE:
Melt-in-the-Mouth Bean Burgers With Sweet Potato Fries (Day 3, Dinner, see page 138)

INGREDIENTS	SWAP SHOP
3 cloves garlic, minced	½ tsp garlic powder
1 onion, finely sliced	–
2cm fresh ginger, minced	½ tsp ground ginger
1 tbsp olive oil	–
salt and pepper	–
1 tsp tikka spice	1 tsp tandoori spice
1 x 400g tin of chopped tomatoes	
1 chicken stock cube	1 vegetable stock cube
2 x 12-minute Naans (see page 162)	–
2 leftover bean burgers (see page 138)	–
½ chilli, de-seeded and finely sliced (to taste)	¼ tsp chilli flakes (to taste)

1. Make the masala curry by adding the garlic, onion and ginger to a saucepan along with the olive oil and a good pinch of salt. Cook over a medium heat for 10 minutes, stirring occasionally.

2. Add the tikka spice, chopped tomatoes and stock cube. Stir together to dissolve the stock cube, then gently simmer over a medium-low heat for 20 minutes.

3. Meanwhile, follow the instructions on page 162 to make two 12-minute Naans. When they are cool, cut them into slices.

4. Place the leftover bean burgers in a non-stick frying pan over a medium-low heat. Cook for 3–4 minutes on one side, then flip them over to cook on the other side for another 3–4 minutes.

5. Divide the masala sauce between two bowls, add the bean burgers and naan slices. Garnish with the chilli, and serve.

ADDITION

2 tbsp coriander, leaves only

HERBY ROAST VEGETABLE RISOTTO

SERVES 2 | READY IN 35 MINS

COOK ONCE EAT TWICE:

Parmesan Breadcrumb Risotto Cakes
(Day 5, Lunch, see page 147)

INGREDIENTS

150g mushrooms
1 courgette, cut into 2cm cubes
300g cherry tomatoes
1 tbsp olive oil
1½ tsp mixed herbs

5 cloves garlic, skin-on
salt and pepper
2 chicken stock cubes
1 tbsp butter
1 onion, diced
400g risotto rice
2 tbsp grated parmesan

SWAP SHOP

1 small aubergine, cubed
300g butternut squash, cubed
300g tomatoes
–
1 tsp dried thyme, oregano
  or rosemary
–
–
2 vegetable stock cubes
–
–
400g paella rice
2 tbsp grated cheddar

Throw in a glass of leftover wine after the onions have cooked and boil for 3 minutes – it adds a gorgeous flavour

1. Put on your kettle to boil and preheat the oven to 200°C (fan 180°C/gas mark 6).

2. If the mushrooms are on the large side, cut them in half. Add them to a large bowl along with the courgette cubes and cherry tomatoes.

3. Add the oil, mixed herbs, four of the skin-on garlic cloves and a good pinch of salt and pepper. Toss together, then tip the whole lot into an oven tray. Transfer to the middle of the oven to roast for 25 minutes.

4. Meanwhile, pour 1.4 litres of boiling water into a jug or bowl. Add the stock cubes and allow them to dissolve.

5. Peel and mince the final clove of garlic. Add the butter to a deep saucepan and fry the onion and garlic over a medium-low heat for 5 minutes. Add a pinch of salt and the risotto rice. Stir together for a minute, then add one quarter of the chicken stock.

6. Stir frequently over a medium heat while adding another quarter of the stock each time the rice has been absorbed by the liquid. You may not need all the stock, so taste-test the rice after 20 minutes. If it is soft with a very slight bite, the risotto is cooked.

7. When the roasted vegetables are ready, remove the whole garlic cloves and squash them with the back of a knife until the soft garlic paste comes out. Discard the skin and stir the paste into the risotto. Set aside half the risotto rice for tomorrow's lunch (Day 5, Lunch, see page 147).

8. Add half of the roast vegetables and season with black pepper. Set aside the remaining half of the roast vegetables for tomorrow's lunch (Day 5, Lunch, see page 147).

9. Stir the parmesan into the risotto and leave it to rest for 2 minutes with a lid on before serving.

ADDITION TO THE ROAST VEGETABLES
1 red chilli, left whole

DINNER

BREAKFAST

LUNCH

DINNER

PEACH CLAFOUTIS WITH GREEK YOGHURT

SERVES 2 | READY IN 10 MINS | VEGETARIAN

INGREDIENTS

2–3 peaches, de-stoned and
  roughly chopped
1 tbsp vegetable oil
2 eggs
120ml whole milk
1 tbsp caster sugar
pinch of salt
50g plain flour
icing sugar, for dusting (optional)
2 tbsp Greek yoghurt

SWAP SHOP

1 x 270g tin of peach halves
  or other fruit
–
–
120ml water
1 tbsp honey
–
50g self-raising flour
–
–

EQUIPMENT

18–21cm round ovenproof
dish or 30cm rectangular
ovenproof dish

If you're short on time, make this the night before and eat in the morning

1. Preheat the oven to 240ºC (fan 220ºC/gas mark 8) and place the ovenproof dish on the middle shelf.

2. Place the fruit in a small saucepan and gently simmer for 3–6 minutes, or until the juice has reduced by three-quarters and has become a syrup.

3. Meanwhile, pour the oil into the hot dish and carefully swirl the oil around to coat the bottom and sides. Return it to the oven to heat the oil.

4. Crack the eggs into a large bowl and add the milk, sugar and salt. Whisk together until combined and then add the flour. Whisk vigorously until a smooth batter has formed.

5. Working quickly, add the fruit to the oven dish, leaving a gap of at least 2–3cm between each piece. Pour the batter over the top and bake in the middle of the oven for 6 minutes.

6. Reduce the temperature to 200ºC (fan 180ºC/gas mark 6) and cook for a further 10 minutes, until risen with a golden top. Times may vary depending on your oven, so keep an eye on it.

7. Dust with icing sugar, if you like, and serve with the hot fruit syrup and a spoonful of Greek yoghurt.

ADDITION

1 tsp vanilla essence

PARMESAN BREADCRUMB RISOTTO CAKES

SERVES 2 | READY IN 15 MINS

COOK ONCE EAT TWICE:
Herby Roast Vegetable Risotto
(Day 4, Dinner, see page 142)

INGREDIENTS

2 slices of bread
25g parmesan, grated
salt and pepper
200g leftover risotto (see
  page 142)
2 tbsp olive oil
portion of leftover roast
  vegetables (see page 142)

EQUIPMENT

food processor or
standing blender

SWAP SHOP

2 slices of any bread
25g gran padano cheese, grated
–
–

–

300g roasted cherry
  tomatoes

1. Blitz both slices of bread into breadcrumbs using a food processor or blender.

2. Transfer the breadcrumbs to a plate, then mix through the parmesan and a good pinch of salt and pepper.

3. Take a portion of risotto (just bigger than golf-ball size) and press it flat in your hand to make a burger shape, around 1cm thick. Coat the cake in the parmesan breadcrumbs by carefully pressing it onto the mixture, then repeat with the remaining risotto. Place the risotto cakes on a plate, ready to cook.

4. Heat 1 tablespoon of the olive oil in a non-stick frying pan over a medium-hot heat. Transfer the risotto cakes to the pan and pan-fry for 3–4 minutes on each side, until golden.

5. Heat the leftover roast vegetables in the microwave, or enjoy cold, drizzled with the remaining olive oil, salt and pepper.

ADDITIONS

2 tbsp basil leaves / 2 tbsp oregano, chopped

GNOCCHI WITH SPINACH AND PESTO

SERVES 2 | READY IN 5 MINS

INGREDIENTS

500g gnocchi
salt and pepper
handful of spinach leaves
4 tbsp Pesto (see
  page 158)

SWAP SHOP

2 portions of spaghetti
–
handful of rocket
–

1. Put on your kettle to boil and fill a large deep saucepan.

2. Add the gnocchi to the saucepan with a pinch of salt. Simmer for 2 minutes until the gnocchi rises to the surface, then drain and add back to the empty saucepan.

3. Add a handful of spinach to the gnocchi with the pesto.

4. Season with pepper and serve immediately.

ADDITIONS

2 tsp pine nuts / 2 tsp flaked almonds
1 tbsp grated parmesan

BREAKFAST

LUNCH

DINNER

CHOCOLATE-DIPPED FRUIT

SERVES 2 | READY IN 15 MINS | VEGETARIAN

INGREDIENTS

75g dark chocolate,
  finely chopped
2 oranges, peeled
2 bananas, peeled and
  chopped into 3 pieces

SWAP SHOP

75g milk chocolate,
  finely chopped
–
–

Try cutting a whole peeled orange in half and dunking it into the chocolate

1. Put on your kettle to boil. Fill a saucepan with boiling water.

2. Place a heatproof bowl on top of the saucepan, making sure that the base of the bowl does not touch the water. Turn the heat to medium-low to keep the water hot but not boiling.

3. Place the chocolate in the bowl and stir until melted.

4. Dip the orange segments and banana pieces into the chocolate, transferring them to dry on a sheet of baking paper (or a plate).

5. Place the fruit in the fridge to set for 10 minutes, or leave to set overnight.

LENTIL SALAD WITH HALLOUMI, MUSHROOMS AND SPINACH

SERVES 2 | READY IN 10 MINS | VEGETARIAN

INGREDIENTS

1 x 400g tin of lentils
125g halloumi
1 tsp olive oil
2 tbsp butter
300g mushrooms, cut into
  quarters
1 clove garlic, minced
1 spring onion, finely chopped
salt and pepper
½ red onion, finely chopped
handful of spinach leaves,
  roughly chopped

SWAP SHOP

250g cooked lentils
125g feta or goat's cheese
–
2 tbsp olive oil
1 courgette, cut into
  2–3cm pieces
–
–
–
½ onion, finely chopped
handful of watercress,
  roughly chopped

1. Rinse the lentils under cold running water, then drain well and add to a large bowl.

2. Slice the halloumi into 5mm strips, then tear it into 2–3cm widths. Heat the olive oil in a non-stick frying pan over a medium heat and fry the halloumi pieces for 1–2 minutes until the underside is golden. Turn the halloumi over and fry for another minute, then add it to the lentils.

3. Melt the butter in the frying pan over a medium-high heat. Add the mushrooms, garlic and spring onion and toss and turn them for 1–2 minutes so they heat through but remain firm. Season well with salt and pepper, then add them to the lentils.

4. Add the red onion and a handful of chopped spinach. Toss together and serve.

ROAST ROOT VEGETABLE TRAY BAKE

SERVES 2 | READY IN 1 HR

COOK ONCE EAT TWICE:
Country Veg Soup
(Day 7, Lunch, see page 153)

INGREDIENTS

300g baby potatoes, halved
  lengthways
500g parsnips,
  halved lengthways
500g carrots,
  halved lengthways
2 turnips, peeled and each cut
  into 8 wedges
3 red onions, cut into quarters
6 cloves garlic, skin-on
3 tbsp olive oil
salt and pepper
4 eggs
2 tbsp Pesto
  (see page 158; optional)
handful of spinach leaves
grated parmesan, to serve

SWAP SHOP

300g potatoes, cut into
  4cm cubes
500g swede,
  halved lengthways
500g beetroot,
  halved lengthways
250g brussels sprouts,
  left whole
3 onions, cut into quarters
–
–
–
–
–
handful of watercress
–

1. Preheat the oven to 200°C (fan 180°C/gas mark 6).

2. Add the vegetables to the oven tray with the garlic and the olive oil. Generously season with salt and pepper and toss it all together. Transfer a third of the mixture to a smaller oven tray.

3. Place both of the trays on a lower shelf of the oven for 45 minutes. Check after 30 minutes, and turn any vegetables that look as if they might burn.

4. After 40 minutes, carefully crack four eggs over the vegetables in the large oven tray. Return the tray to the oven for 5 minutes, until the egg white has set.

5. Serve the contents of the larger tray with the Pesto, if using, a handful of spinach leaves and grated parmesan. Reserve the smaller tray of roast vegetables for tomorrow's lunch: Country Veg Soup (Day 7, Lunch, see page 153).

LUNCH

BREAKFAST

ENGLISH BREAKFAST IN A YORKSHIRE

SERVES 2 | READY IN 25 MINS

INGREDIENTS

1 tbsp vegetable oil, plus 1 tsp
4 eggs
120ml whole milk
salt and pepper
50g plain flour
½ tbsp butter
1 courgette, cut into 2–3cm cubes
½ clove garlic (optional), minced
4 rashers of bacon
1 spring onion, finely chopped
1 large tomato, halved

SWAP SHOP

–
–
–
–
50g self-raising flour
–
150g mushrooms, left whole
–
6 sundried tomatoes
1 tbsp chopped chives
–

EQUIPMENT

18–21cm ovenproof dish

Sundried tomato makes an excellent swap for bacon

1. Preheat the oven to 240ºC (fan 220ºC/gas mark 8). Add 1 tablespoon of the oil to the oven dish and place it in the oven.

2. In a large bowl, whisk together two of the eggs, the milk and a pinch of salt. Add the flour and whisk until a smooth batter has formed.

3. Working quickly, remove the dish from the oven and swirl the oil to coat the sides. Pour in the batter and cook for 6 minutes, then lower the temperature to 200ºC (fan 180ºC/gas mark 6). Cook for 10–15 minutes until golden.

4. Meanwhile, melt the butter in a large pan over a medium heat and add the courgette, garlic, if using, and a pinch of salt and pepper. Stir and cook for 6–10 minutes, until al dente.

5. Heat the remaining 1 teaspoon of oil in a non-stick frying pan over a medium heat. Fry the bacon for 3 minutes and then move it to one side of the pan. Crack the remaining eggs into the frying pan and season with salt and pepper. Add in the spring onion. Flip the bacon, add the tomato to the pan, then fry together until the egg has set.

6. Remove the Yorkshire pudding from the oven and add your fillings. Serve up and share.

ADDITIONS

2 sausages / black pudding / 1 tin of baked beans

COUNTRY VEG SOUP

SERVES 2 | READY IN 1 HR 15 MINS

COOK ONCE EAT TWICE:

Roast Root Vegetable Tray Bake
(Day 6, Dinner, see page 151)

INGREDIENTS

1 tsp olive oil
1 onion, diced
2 cloves garlic, minced
leftover Roast Root Vegetable Tray
  Bake (see page 151)
1 chicken stock cube
1 tsp mixed herbs
salt and pepper

SWAP SHOP

–
–
–
–

1 vegetable stock cube
1 tsp rosemary
–

EQUIPMENT

stick blender

1. Add the oil to a large saucepan and fry the onion and garlic over a medium-low heat for 5 minutes. Put on your kettle to boil.

2. Add the leftover root vegetables to the pan and sauté for another 5 minutes.

3. Pour 800ml boiling water into the saucepan along with the stock cube and mixed herbs. Bring to the boil, stir and gently simmer for 10 minutes.

4. Blitz together with a stick blender until smooth. Taste test and season with salt and pepper as necessary, and serve.

ADDITIONS

handful of cheese croutons / 2 tsp lemon juice
1 tsp chilli flakes / 1 tbsp sage leaves, fried

BEEF IN FIVE SPICE

SERVES 2 | READY IN 1 HR 15 MINS

INGREDIENTS

350–500g beef brisket,
  cut into wafer-thin pieces
2 tbsp olive oil
3 cloves garlic, sliced
1cm fresh ginger, minced
3 spring onions, finely chopped
½ chilli, de-seeded and
  finely chopped (optional)
salt and pepper
1½ tsp Chinese five spice
1 x 400g tin of chopped tomatoes
1 chicken stock cube
1 tsp caster sugar (optional)
200g rice
2 tbsp coriander, leaves only

SWAP SHOP

350–500g beef roasting joint,
  cut into wafer-thin pieces
–
1 tsp garlic powder
¼ tsp ground ginger
–
¼ tsp chilli flakes (optional)

–

–
–
300g tomatoes, chopped
1 beef stock cube
–
200g cous cous
2 tbsp parsley, chopped

Slice the meat wafer thin to speed up the cooking process and improve the flavour

1. Place the slices of beef in a large saucepan full of cold water over a medium-hot heat.

2. Bring to the boil and let it bubble away for 2 minutes, then drain the beef and rinse it thoroughly under running cold water. Reserve the meat for later in the recipe.

3. Rinse the saucepan and return it to the heat. Add the oil along with the garlic, ginger, two-thirds of the chopped spring onions, chilli, if using, and a pinch of salt. Fry over a medium-high heat for 2 minutes, then add the beef slices and Chinese five spice. Fry for another 2 minutes.

4. Add the chopped tomatoes, stock cube and sugar, if using. Stir well, pour in 200ml water and bring to the boil. Simmer for 1 hour, stirring occasionally.

5. With 15 minutes to go, put on your kettle to boil. Add the rice to a saucepan and fill it with boiling water. Cook until done, then drain and bring to the table.

6. Garnish the beef with the coriander and the remaining chopped spring onion.

ADDITIONS

1 tsp Szechuan pepper / 1 tsp coriander seeds

DINNER

PESTO

MAKES 400G | READY IN 5 MINS

INGREDIENTS

20g basil
50g parmesan

200g cream cheese
1 clove garlic
4 handfuls of spinach leaves

4 tbsp olive oil
salt and pepper

SWAP SHOP

20g oregano
50g grana padano
  (hard cheese)
200g ricotta cheese
–
4 handfuls of blanched stinging
  nettle leaves
–
–

EQUIPMENT
stick blender

1. Remove and discard the basil stalks. Add the basil leaves to a large deep bowl with the rest of the ingredients and use the stick blender to pulse it all together until smooth. Season with salt and pepper to taste.

2. Keep refrigerated in a closed container or jar for 4–5 days.

HUMMUS

MAKES 400G | READY IN 5 MINS | VEGETARIAN

INGREDIENTS

1 x 400g tin of chickpeas, drained
  and rinsed
2 tbsp olive oil, plus extra
  for drizzling
juice of ½ lemon
1 tbsp tahini paste (optional)
½ clove garlic
½ tsp salt

SWAP SHOP

1 x 400g tin of butterbeans,
  drained and rinsed
2 tbsp sundried tomato oil,
  plus extra for drizzling
juice of ½ lime
–
¾ tsp garlic powder
–

EQUIPMENT
stick blender

1. Add the chickpeas to a deep large bowl. Pour in 2 tablespoons of water along with the olive oil and lemon juice.

2. Add the tahini paste (if using), garlic, and salt. Use the stick blender to pulse it all together until smooth. Drizzle with olive oil. Keep refrigerated in an airtight container or jar for 2–3 days.

ADDITION
½ tsp ground coriander / ¼ tsp paprika

SPICED TOMATO CHUTNEY

MAKES 350G | READY IN 1 HOUR | VEGETARIAN

INGREDIENTS

1 tsp olive oil
1 apple, peeled and
    cut into cubes
1 onion, finely chopped
2 cloves garlic, minced
1 tsp tandoori spice
300g cherry tomatoes
salt and pepper

SWAP SHOP

–
3 plums, cut into cubes

–
½ tsp garlic powder
1 tsp tikka spice
300g tomatoes, cubed
–

1. Heat the olive oil in a saucepan over a medium heat along with the apple, onion and garlic. Throw in the tandoori spice, cherry tomatoes, a good pinch of salt and pepper and 200ml water.

2. Bring the mixture to the boil, then reduce to a bubbling simmer for 45 minutes, stirring occasionally.

3. Allow to cool before placing in a clean jar or airtight container. Keep refrigerated for 6–7 days.

Perfect for mezzes, sandwiches and naan bread

THAI GREEN CURRY PASTE

MAKES 100G | READY IN 10 MINS | VEGETARIAN

INGREDIENTS

2 lemongrass stalks
100g bunch of coriander, stalks
    and leaves roughly chopped
3cm fresh ginger, roughly chopped
1 small onion, roughly chopped
10 cloves garlic, roughly chopped
2–4 green chillies, de-seeded and
    roughly chopped
1 tbsp butter
1½ tbsp salt

SWAP SHOP

3cm lime peel
–

–

–

–

2–4 red chillies, de-seeded
    and roughly chopped
1 tbsp olive oil
1 chicken stock cube

EQUIPMENT
stick blender

1. Remove the ends and discard the outer one or two leaves from the lemongrass. Chop the rest into 2cm pieces and add to a deep bowl.

2. Add the coriander, ginger, onion, garlic and chillies to the bowl.

3. Throw in the butter, 3 tablespoons of water and salt and then blitz with a stick blender until a paste has formed.

4. Keep the fresh paste in a jar in the fridge for up to 7 days, or freeze portions in an ice-cube tray for up to 3 months. Defrost in the microwave, or on a low heat in a pan.

12-MINUTE NAANS

MAKES 2 NAANS | READY IN 12 MINS | VEGETARIAN

INGREDIENTS

200g self-raising flour,
   plus 2 tbsp for dusting
salt and pepper
2 tbsp olive oil
2 tbsp coriander, roughly chopped,
   plus extra for garnish (optional)

SWAP SHOP

200g plain flour, plus
   2 tbsp for dusting
–
1 tbsp butter
–

1. Put on your kettle to boil.

2. Pour the flour into a large bowl along with a good pinch of salt, 1 tablespoon of the olive oil and chopped coriander, if using. Pour 175ml boiling water over the flour mixture and stir with a fork until a soft dough has formed.

3. Take the dough out of the bowl and knead it on a flat surface for 1 minute until combined and smooth. It will feel lovely and warm on your hands.

4. Split the dough into two balls. Sprinkle 2 tablespoons of flour onto the kitchen surface and roll out two 20–25cm long tear-shaped naans, about 5mm thick. Add more flour to stop any sticking, and use a wine bottle if you don't have a rolling pin!

5. Drizzle 1 teaspoon of oil onto each naan, season with a pinch of salt and pepper and some chopped coriander (if using).

6. As if pretending to type on a keyboard, create multiple dimples all over the surface of each naan.

7. Heat up the grill to its hottest temperature. Transfer the naans to a wire oven rack, oil-side up. Grill for 4–6 minutes until golden, then flip and grill on the other side for another 2 minutes. Keep an eye on the naans so that they do not burn. Serve fresh.

SOY TAHINI DRESSING

MAKES 50ML | READY IN 5 MINS | VEGETARIAN

INGREDIENTS

1½ tbsp tahini paste
1½ tbsp soy sauce
pinch of chilli flakes
  (optional)

SWAP SHOP

1½ tbsp peanut butter
–
–

Delicious over lightly steamed broccoli or other veg

1. Add the tahini paste, soy sauce and 3 tablespoons of water into a clean jar. Use a fork to loosen the tahini paste, then put the lid on and vigorously shake until a smooth silky sauce has formed.

2. Add a pinch of chilli flakes if you like things spicy. Keep refrigerated in an airtight container or jar for 6–7 days in the fridge.

PEANUT SATAY SAUCE

MAKES 200G | READY IN 10 MINS | VEGETARIAN

INGREDIENTS

100g peanuts
100ml coconut milk
1 tsp tandoori spice
3 cloves garlic, minced
2cm fresh ginger, minced
1 tbsp lime juice
1 tbsp coriander stalks
salt

SWAP SHOP

100g cashew nuts
–
1 tsp tikka spice
–
–
1 tbsp lemon juice
1 tsp ground coriander
–

EQUIPMENT
stick blender

1. Add the peanuts, coconut milk and tandoori spice into a small saucepan. Bring to the boil and simmer for 5 minutes.

2. Add the garlic, ginger, lime juice, coriander stalks and 100ml water. Blitz with a stick blender until smooth.

3. Taste test and season with a good pinch of salt, if necessary. Keep refrigerated in an airtight container or jar for 2–3 days.

GRANOLA

MAKES 600G | READY IN 45 MINS | VEGETARIAN

INGREDIENTS

150–200g dried fruit and
 nut mixture
400g porridge oats
¾ tsp salt
170ml honey
100g sugar
120ml vegetable oil
1 tsp vanilla essence (optional)

SWAP SHOP

150–200g any seed, nut
 and fruit mixture
–
–
170ml maple syrup
100g date sugar
120ml coconut oil
–

1. Preheat the oven to 180°C (fan 160°C/ gas mark 4).

2. Place the fruit and nut mixture into a plastic food bag and beat with a rolling pin or the back of a pan to break it into small pieces.

3. Combine the broken mixture with the porridge oats and salt. Spread it all evenly across an oven tray.

4. Pour the honey, sugar, vegetable oil and vanilla essence (if using) into a saucepan over a medium heat and bring to the boil. Keep an eye on it, and when the liquid starts to foam, carefully and evenly pour it over the oat mixture.

5. Stir the whole thing together with a spoon to coat the oats. Bake it in the oven for 25–30 minutes, gently stirring once after 10 minutes and again after 20 minutes, until the oats are golden.

6. Remove the granola from the oven and allow to cool before storing in an airtight container for up to 4 weeks.

Cooking breakfast from scratch makes your money go further

QUICK
BREAKFASTS
and Desserts

BLACK BEAN, SWEETCORN, TOMATO AND CHILLI TOAST

SERVES 2 | READY IN 7 MINS | VEGETARIAN

INGREDIENTS	SWAP SHOP
1 x 400g tin of black beans, drained	–
200g tinned sweetcorn, drained	–
1 tsp olive oil	–
salt and pepper	–
1 tsp tandoori spice	1 tsp tikka spice
1 tomato, diced	2–3 cherry tomatoes, diced
½ spring onion, finely chopped	–
2 tbsp grated cheddar	–
1 handful of spinach leaves	–
2 pieces of toast	2 plain tortilla wraps

1. Add the black beans and sweetcorn to a frying pan over a medium-hot heat along with the olive oil, a good pinch of salt and pepper and the tandoori spice. Heat through for 2 minutes then remove from the heat.

2. Stir through the tomato, spring onion and grated cheddar.

3. Add a few spinach leaves to each piece of toast, then add the topping. Serve.

CHEESY EGGS AND AVOCADO TOAST

SERVES 2 | READY IN 7 MINS | VEGETARIAN

INGREDIENTS	SWAP SHOP
4 eggs	–
2 tsp butter	–
salt and pepper	–
2 tbsp grated cheddar	–
½ avocado, peeled, de-stoned and sliced	–
1 tomato, diced	–
2 pieces of toast	2 plain tortilla wraps

1. Crack four eggs into a large bowl and whisk them together.

2. Melt the butter in a non-stick frying pan over a medium-low heat and pour in the eggs. Leave for 30 seconds, then using a spatula, gently push and pull the eggs around the pan until no more liquid egg is present and soft curds are formed.

3. Remove from the heat, season well with salt and pepper and gently stir through the cheddar.

4. Share the eggs, avocado and tomato between the two pieces of toast and serve.

FRUIT, HONEY AND YOGHURT TOAST

SERVES 2 | READY IN 7 MINS | VEGETARIAN

INGREDIENTS

2 tbsp Greek yoghurt
2 pieces of toast
4 tbsp Granola (see page 166)
2 ripe bananas, sliced

2 tbsp honey

SWAP SHOP

2 tbsp crème fraiche
–
4 tbsp dried fruit and nut mix
¼ pineapple, sliced or
   10 strawberries, halved
2 tbsp melted chocolate

1. Spread 1 tablespoon of Greek yoghurt on each piece of toast, followed by 2 tablespoons of granola and slices of ripe banana.

2. Drizzle with the honey and serve.

AVOCADO, SUNDRIED TOMATO AND CHICKPEA TOAST WITH SPINACH AND FETA

SERVES 2 | READY IN 7 MINS | VEGETARIAN

INGREDIENTS

1 x 400g tin of chickpeas, drained

3 tsp olive oil

salt and pepper

3 sundried tomatoes, finely chopped

1 handful of spinach leaves, shredded

½ avocado, peeled, de-stoned and diced

¼ pepper (any colour), finely diced

50g feta, crumbled

1 tsp lemon juice

2 pieces of toast

SWAP SHOP

1 x 400g tin of cannellini beans, drained

–

–

8 olives, finely chopped

1 handful of kale, shredded

1 tomato, finely diced

–

50g goat's cheese, crumbled

–

2 plain tortilla wraps

1. Add the chickpeas to a medium-hot frying pan along with the olive oil and a good pinch of salt and pepper.

2. Add the sundried tomatoes and spinach to the pan and toss together to wilt the spinach, then remove from the heat.

3. Add the avocado and pepper to the chickpeas along with the crumbled feta and gently toss together with the lemon juice. Pile on top of the two pieces of toast and serve.

Desserts

SHORTCRUST PASTRY TART CASE

**MAKES 1 SHORTCRUST PASTRY CASE |
READY IN 20 MINS**

INGREDIENTS

200g plain flour, plus 2 tbsp extra
 for dusting
125g cold butter

SWAP SHOP

–

125ml vegetable oil

EQUIPMENT
18–21cm tart tin

This is also perfect for savoury tarts

1. Preheat the oven to 200°C (fan 180°C/
gas mark 6).

2. Add the flour to a mixing bowl. Grate
or chop the cold butter into the bowl and
use your hands to rub the butter and flour
together until it looks like fine breadcrumbs.

3. Add 2 tablespoons of cold water into the
bowl and mix together to form a dough.
Do not knead the dough, but firmly press it
into a soft ball.

4. Dust the work surface with the flour and
roll out the dough until 5mm thick, and 2cm
larger than your tart tin. Carefully transfer
the dough to the tin and lightly press up the
sides. Cut off any overhanging dough.

5. Prick the base 20 times with a fork and
bake in the middle of the oven for 16 minutes.
Traditionally, the dough would be lined with
parchment and weighed down with ceramic
baking beans, but it's not strictly necessary.

6. When the tart case has been blind-baked,
take it out of the oven and fill it with a sweet
or savoury filling. Bake again according to
recipe guidelines. You can also allow the
blind-baked shortcrust pastry to cool, then
wrap it in foil and freeze it for up to
1 month.

WHIPPED CHOCOLATE TART

**SERVES 4 | READY IN 20 MINS
PLUS TART CASE (IF MAKING)**

INGREDIENTS

1 x Shortcrust Pastry Tart Case
  (see opposite)
4 egg whites
pinch of salt
100g dark chocolate, roughly
  chopped
4 tbsp caster sugar
6 tbsp whole milk
ice cream or Greek yoghurt
  (optional)

EQUIPMENT

18–21cm tart tin

SWAP SHOP

20cm shop-bought pastry
  tart case
–
–
100g milk chocolate, roughly
  chopped
–
6 tbsp double cream
–

Save the egg yolks in the fridge overnight and enjoy them for breakfast. Poach them for 1–2 minutes and serve with toast

1. Put on your kettle to boil and preheat the oven to 200°C (fan 180°C/gas mark 6).

2. Make the Shortcrust Pastry Tart Case opposite or use a shop-bought one.

3. Add the egg whites and salt to a mixing bowl. Vigorously whisk the egg whites with a balloon whisk or hand-held electric whisk until stiff peaks are formed.

4. Pour 4–5cm boiling water into a saucepan and rest a heatproof bowl on top of the pan over a medium-low heat. Make sure the base of the bowl doesn't touch the water. Add 80g of the roughly chopped chocolate into the bowl. Keep the water gently simmering and stir the chocolate until melted.

5. Add the sugar and milk to the melted chocolate, and carefully remove the bowl from the pan. Whisk together to combine the milk and chocolate. Cool for 30 seconds then pour the mixture into the egg whites and very gently whisk until combined.

6. Scatter the remaining chocolate evenly across the blind-baked tart case. Pour the whisked chocolate filling over the top and bake in the middle of the oven for exactly 14 minutes.

7. When the tart is ready, the middle should be wobbly and will remain soft as it cools. Serve with ice cream or Greek yoghurt, if you fancy it.

GLAZED APPLE TART

**SERVES 4 | READY IN 25 MINS
PLUS TART CASE (IF MAKING)**

INGREDIENTS

1 x Shortcrust Pastry Tart Case
   (see page 176)
1 x 400g tin of apricot halves in
   light syrup
3 apples, cored and cut into
   quarters
1 tbsp caster sugar
ice cream or Greek yoghurt
   (optional)

EQUIPMENT
18–21cm tart tin
stick blender

SWAP SHOP

20cm shop-bought pastry
   tart case
–
–
–
–

1. Preheat the oven to 200ºC (fan 180ºC/ gas mark 6).

2. Make the Shortcrust Pastry Tart Case on page 176 or use a shop-bought one.

3. Drain the tin of apricots over a small saucepan and set the fruit aside. Simmer the syrup in the pan until only 1 tablespoon of liquid remains, then remove it from the heat.

4. Meanwhile, add the apricot halves to a large bowl and blitz with a stick blender into a smooth puree. Pour the puree into the blind-baked tart case and spread it out evenly.

5. Slice the apple quarters into ultra-thin 1–3mm pieces. Starting from the outside edge of the tart, place the slices along the perimeter. Once the circle is complete, lay another circle along the smaller diameter, and repeat until a small circle remains in the middle.

6. Sprinkle the sugar over the apples and bake in the middle oven for 15 minutes.

7. If the syrup has cooled and solidified, add a few drops of water and re-heat until liquid. Pour the syrup over the apples and return to the oven for another 5 minutes. Serve hot or cold with ice cream or Greek yoghurt, if you fancy it.

ORANGE CAKE

SERVES 6–8 | READY IN 35 MINS

INGREDIENTS

	SWAP SHOP
115g butter, plus extra for greasing	–
230g caster sugar	–
3 eggs	–
115g plain flour, plus 1 tsp	–
1 tsp baking powder	–
zest of 1 orange	–
juice of 3 oranges	–

EQUIPMENT
21cm non-stick cake tin

1. Preheat the oven to 200°C (fan 180°C/gas mark 6).

2. Melt the butter in a large saucepan over a low heat. When it is melted, remove the pan from the heat and add 115g of the sugar.

3. One by one, add the eggs, mixing each one in before adding the next. Add the plain flour, baking powder, half the orange zest and the juice of 1 orange. Stir together until all is combined and the consistency is smooth.

4. Grease the cake tin with a little butter and throw in the extra teaspoon of flour. Tip and rotate the tin so that the flour coats it, then pour in the cake batter and bake for 25 minutes in the middle of the oven.

5. Meanwhile, add the remaining orange zest, juice and sugar to a bowl. Stir until the sugar has dissolved.

6. When the cake has baked, remove it from the oven and place a plate over the top of the tin. Tip the cake onto the plate, then place a flat serving plate on top of the cake base and flip it again so that the cake faces up and the tin can be removed.

7. Slowly spoon 1 tablespoon of the orange syrup over the top of the cake and gently rub it in with the back of the spoon until it is completely absorbed. Repeat with rest of the syrup to create a beautifully moist orange cake. Serve.

INDEX

Note: page numbers in **bold** refer to photographs.

ABOUT LIMAHL

. . . .

Limahl Asmall has spent the past ten years cooking quick and
tasty meals – first in kitchens in Edinburgh, and more recently as a street-food
chef in London. He is founder of the Tiny Budget Cooking website,
which was inspired by his own experience and the needs of an increasing
number of people to cook on a limited budget. The website has garnered
attention for its authentic and inclusive approach to cooking, and features a free
downloadable mealplan, helping those on low incomes to have access to varied
meals in minutes. It was included in the BBC Radio 4 Food Programme's
Cookbooks of 2016. This is his first printed book.

ACKNOWLEDGEMENTS

. . . .

Look Mum, I've got a cookbook! Thank you for that conversation a
couple years ago that lit the fire in me, and to my family for fanning
the flames. To my inspirational editors and agent, Carole, Martha and
Clare, it's a dream to work with you, and to the photography and
food stylist team lead by Charlotte and Kate, I enjoyed every minute.
Your bunches of flowers (coriander) are in the post.

Thank you to everyone who believes in my mission to make great food
achievable for all, and a special thank you to Tiphaine whose love and
support has made this book possible. As you say, the happiest people don't
have the best of everything; they make the best of everything.

USEFUL WEBSITES

. . . .

www.tinybudgetcooking.com/lists
Print off the weekly shopping lists to take to
your supermarket.

www.tinybudgetcooking.com/reduced
Find out when supermarkets discount their
produce.

www.tinybudgetcooking.com/goodthings
There's some awesome social giving campaigns running alongside this
cookbook – head to my website to see the impact of our work.

www.eatseasonably.co.uk
Use this interactive calendar to find out when
fruit and veg is season.

First published 2017 by Bluebird
an imprint of Pan Macmillan
20 New Wharf Road, London N1 9RR
Associated companies throughout the world
www.panmacmillan.com

ISBN 978-1-5098-5810-1

A CIP catalogue record for this book is available from the British Library.

Printed and bound in Italy.

Publisher **Carole Tonkinson**
Senior Editor **Martha Burley**
Senior Production Controller **Ena Matagic**
Design **Cabinlondon.co.uk**
Photography **Charlotte Tolhurst**
Prop Styling **Linda Berlin**
Food Styling **Kate Wesson**

Visit **www.panmacmillan.com** to read more about all our books and to buy them.
You will also find features, author interviews and news of any author events,
and you can sign up for e-newsletters so that you're always first to hear about our
new releases.